barcode over.

100 LITERACY HOMEWORK ACTIVITIES

Published by Scholastic Ltd,
Villiers House,
Clarendon Avenue,
Leamington Spa,
Warwickshire CV32 5PR

© **2001 Scholastic Ltd**
Text © David Waugh, Wendy Jolliffe
and Kathleen Taylor 2001
1 2 3 4 5 6 7 8 9   1 2 3 4 5 6 7 8 9 0

British Library Cataloguing-in-Publication Data
A catalogue record of this book is available from the British Library.

ISBN 0-439-01834-X

AUTHORS
David Waugh, Wendy Jolliffe
and Kathleen Taylor
EDITORIAL
Clare Gallaher, Dulcie Booth and
Jeffrey Nosbaum
DESIGN
Crystal Presentations Ltd
COVER DESIGN
Joy Monkhouse
COVER ARTWORK
Adrian Barclay
ILLUSTRATOR
Peter Smith

ACKNOWLEDGEMENTS

The publishers gratefully acknowledge permission to reproduce the following copyright materials:

Curtis Brown, New York for the use of 'Winter Morning' by Ogden Nash © 1962, Ogden Nash (1962, Little Brown).

The Controller of HMSO and the DfEE for the use of extracts from *The National Literacy Strategy: Framework for Teaching* © 1998, Crown Copyright (1998, DfEE, Her Majesty's Stationery Office).

Wendy Jolliffe for the use of 'Sounds of the City' by Wendy Jolliffe © 2001, Wendy Jolliffe, (previously unpublished).

Philip & Tacey Ltd for the use of an extract from 'Sack and the Jeanstalk' from *Some Well-known Tales* © Dee Reid, (1992, Philograph Publications).

Marian Reiner Literary Agent, New York for the use of 'Noses' by Aileen Fisher from *Up the Windy Hill* by Aileen Fisher © 1953, 1981 Aileen Fisher.

Scholastic Inc for the use of 'Books are fun! Books are great!' from *Thematic Poems: Songs and Finger Plays* by Meish Goldish © 1998, Meish Goldish (1998, Scholastic Inc).

Walker Books for the use of 'Fred's Bread' and 'Doctor Deer's Ear and Hearing Clinic' from *Sound City* by Sarah Hayes and illustrated by Margaret Chamberlain © 1998, Sarah Hayes (1998, Walker Books).

Every effort has been made to trace copyright holders and the publishers apologise for any omissions.

100 Literacy Homework Activities: Year 2

3606801020

CONTENTS

100 LITERACY HOMEWORK ACTIVITIES

About the series

100 Literacy Homework Activities is a series of teacher resource books for Years 1–6. Each book is year-specific and provides a core of word-, sentence- and text-level activities within the guidelines for the National Literacy Strategy in England. The content of these activities is also appropriate for and adaptable to the requirements of Primary 1–7 in Scottish schools.

Each book offers three terms of homework activities, matched to the termly planning in the National Literacy Strategy *Framework for Teaching* for that year. Schools in England and Wales that decide not to adopt the National Literacy Strategy will still find the objectives, approaches, content and lesson contexts familiar and valuable. However, the teacher will need to choose from the activities to match specific requirements and planning.

The homework activities provided in the books are intended as a support for the teacher, school literacy co-ordinator or trainee teacher. The series can be used alongside its companion series, *100 Literacy Hours,* or with any scheme of work, as the basis for planning homework activities throughout the school, in line with the school's homework policy. The resources are suitable for use with single or mixed-age classes, single- and mixed-ability groups and for team planning of homework across a year or stage. The teacher may also find the activities valuable for extension work in class or as additional resources for assessment. The teacher can even combine them to create a 'module' – a sequence of lessons on a common skill or theme, for example, by bringing together all the homework sheets on spelling words with the vowel phonemes *oo, ar, oy* and *ow.*

Using the books

The activities in each book are organised by term, then by word-, sentence- and text-level focus and finally by specific National Literacy Strategy objective. Each of the 100 homework activities is comprised of at least one photocopiable page to send home. Each sheet provides instructions for the child and a brief note to the helper (be that a parent, grandparent, neighbour or sibling), stating simply and clearly its purpose and suggesting support and/or a further challenge to offer the child. Every sheet is clearly marked with a W (word), S (sentence) or T (text) symbol to designate its main focus. (Please note that 'they', 'them', 'their' has sometimes been used in the helper and teachers' notes to refer to 'child'. This avoids the 'he or she' construction.)

Some of the pages are designed for writing on; others are not. In the case of the latter – or when children wish to extend their writing – tell them to use the back of the page or a separate piece of paper. If appropriate, extra paper should be given out with the homework activity.

There is a supporting teachers' note for each activity. These notes include:

- **Objective:** the specific learning objective of the homework (referenced to the National Literacy Strategy *Framework for Teaching*).
- **Lesson context:** a brief description of the classroom experience recommended for the children prior to undertaking the homework.
- **Setting the homework:** advice on how to explain the work to the children and set it in context before it is taken home.
- **Differentiation:** where appropriate, advice on how to support the less able and challenge the more able. Most of the resource sheets have been designed with differentiation in mind and it is recommended that the teacher writes appropriate modifications to the general instructions on the reverse of the sheet. Occasionally, a homework sheet is aimed at a particular ability range and in these cases, suggestions for other children are given in the teachers' notes.
- **Back at school:** suggestions on how to respond to the returned homework, such as discussion with the children or specific advice on marking.

Making the most of these resources

The best way to use these homework resources is to use them flexibly, integrating them with a sequence of literacy sessions over a number of days. Such an approach will also ensure that the needs of an individual or groups of children are met in different ways. Some of the homework sheets will be greatly enhanced by enlarging to A3 size as this provides children with more space in which to write. Others, for example, the sets of story cards, lend themselves to being laminated for re-use.

Here are some ideas for different types of use:

Preparation
- Give a word- or sentence-level homework to prepare for a skills session later in the week. This allows the skill to be reviewed in less time, thus leaving more time for group activities.
- Give a text-level homework as a way of preparing for more detailed work on a particular type of text in a future literacy lesson.
- Give work on a particular short text as a preparation for further work on that text or a related text in a future lesson.

Follow-up
- Give a word- or sentence-level homework as a follow-up to a literacy lesson to provide more practice in a particular skill.
- Give a text-level homework as a creative way of responding to work done in a literacy lesson.
- Use one of the many short texts as a follow-up to a study of a similar type of text in a lesson.

Reinforcement
- Give a carefully selected word- or sentence-level homework to specific children who need extra practice.
- Give a text-level homework to specific children to reinforce text-level work done in class.
- Use a short text with specific children to reinforce work done on similar texts.

Supporting your helpers

The importance of involving parents in homework is generally acknowledged. For this reason, as well as the 'Dear Helper' note on each homework sheet, there is also a homework diary sheet on page 128 which can be photocopied and sent home with the homework. Multiple copies of these can be filed or stapled together to make a longer-term homework record. For each activity, there is space to record its title, the date on which it was sent home and spaces for responses to the work from the helper, the child and the teacher. The homework diary is intended to encourage home–school links, so that parents and carers know what is being taught and can make informed comments about their child's progress.

It is also worth writing to parents and helpers, or holding a meeting, to discuss their role. This could include an explanation of how they can support their children's homework, for example, by:
- providing an appropriate space where the child can concentrate and has the necessary resources to hand;
- becoming actively involved by interpreting instructions, helping with problems, sharing reading and participating in the paired activities where required.

Discuss with them how much time you expect the child to spend on the homework. If, after that time, a child is stuck, or has not finished, then suggest to the parent/helper that they should not force the child to continue. Ask them to write an explanation and the teacher will give extra help the next day. However, if children are succeeding at the task and need more time, this can be allowed – but bear in mind that children need a varied and balanced home life!

It is worth discussing with parents what is meant by 'help' as they should be careful that they do not go as far as doing the homework for the child. Legitimate help will include sharing the reading of texts, helping to clarify problems, discussing possible answers, etc., but it is important that the child is at some stage left to do his or her best. The teacher can then form an accurate assessment of the child's strengths and weaknesses and provide suitable follow-up work.

Using the activities with the 100 Literacy Hours series

A cross-referenced grid has been provided (on pages 6 and 7) for those who wish to use these homework activities with the corresponding *100 Literacy Hours* book. The grid suggests if and where a homework task might fit within the context of the appropriate *100 Literacy Hours* unit and there may be more than one appropriate activity. Note that, on some occasions, the best homework will be to continue or finish off the classwork, to read a text, to learn spellings, or to research a topic. Sometimes, the homework page could be used for a skills session in class and one of the resources from *100 Literacy Hours* can be used for homework.

	UNITS IN 100 LITERACY HOURS: Y2		100 LITERACY HOMEWORK ACTIVITIES		
HOUR	PAGE			PAGE	NLS OBJECTIVE
		Term 1			
		Unit	Title		
1	22	**Right This Way**	Play the game	54	T14
2	23		Simon says!	55	T14
1	25	**Label It!**	Label your home	40	W10
2	26		Find it!	41	W10
1	30	**Lost in a Shop**	Lost on the beach	48	T4
2	30		At the seaside	42	W10
3	31		Words we use a lot	34	W5
4	32		What happened and when?	49	T4
5	32		Spelling game	35	W5/9
1	36	**Baking Bread**	Reading instructions	50	T13
2	37		Writing instructions	56	T15
3	37		Cleaning your teeth	44	S2/T14/16
1	42	**Charlie's a Good Boy Now!**	Matching sounds	28	W3
2	42		Choose the right word	43	S1
3	43		Match it!	29	W3
4	43		Odd one out	31	W4
5	44		Down town	30	W3
1	50	**Monday's Child**	Solomon Grundy	36	W5/9/10
1	54	**Rhyming Lines**	Months of the year	37	W5/10
2	55		One to ten	32	W4
3	56		Number rhymes	33	W4
1	59	**An Alphabetical Story**	Spell it!	38	W9
2	60		Alphabetical order	39	W9
1	63	**Game Time**	How to play 'Concentration'	51	T13/W5
2	64		Hide and seek	58	T15/18
3	64		Stick in the mud	52	T13/7
4	65		Write your own instructions	59	T15/18
5	65		Getting to school	60	T15/16/18
1	70	**Chloe and Jack**	Jill and Jack	46	S5/T1
2	70		Find the capitals	47	S5
3	71		Punctuate the passage	45	S4
1	74	**What's Cooking?**	Making a pancake	53	T13/W10
2	75		Write your own recipe	57	T15
		Term 2			
1	78	**Chloe Confused**	Charlotte, Charles and Chloe	64	W3
2	79		Chef's chocolate	65	W3
1	82	**Sneezles/Waiting at the Window**	What a collection!	66	W3
2	84		Time to rhyme	67	W3
1	87	**My Shadow**	Winter morning	88	T11
1	92	**Words within Words**	Word sums	68	W4
2	93		Making compounds words	69	W4
3	93		Find the compound words	70	W4
1	96	**Bedtime and Four Apples Fall**	Midnight adventure	62	W2
2	98		Words for all	63	W2
1	101	**Syllables**	How many syllables?	71	W5
2	102		Matching syllables	72	W5
1	104	**Who am I?**	What's black & white and read all over?	79	S6
2	104		Stop throwing paint!	76	S1
3	105		Make a speech!	80	S6
1	108	**The Rescue**	Noses	90	T11/8
1	112	**Little Red Riding Hood**	Ooh, look at that!	61	W1

HOUR	PAGE	UNITS IN 100 LITERACY HOURS: Y2	Title	PAGE	NLS OBJECTIVE
		Term 2	100 LITERACY HOMEWORK ACTIVITIES		
		Unit	Title		
2	113		Character sketches	86	T6/14
3	113		Descriptions	82	S9/T6
4	113		Adjectives for Andrew	83	S9/T6
5	114		Who said that?	78	S5
1	117	Getting Ready for School	Shopping at the supermarket	92	T21
2	118		Make your own flow chart	93	T21
1	121	Swimming after School	Opposites	74	W11/8
2	122		Find the opposite	75	W11/8
3	122		Changing sentences	81	S9/W11
4	123		Two different people?	84	S9/W11/T14
1	127	What is Red?	Hands	87	T8/10/11
2	128		Books are great!	89	T11
3	129		Write a poem	91	T15
1	132	A Funny Thing Happened	Missing mouse	85	T4
2	132		The secret garden in the city	73	W6
3	133		Painting	77	S1
		Term 3			
1	140	Tongue-Twisters	Alliterative sentences	120	T11
2	141		Sounds of the city	97	W1
1	144	Jack and the Beanstalk	Sack and the Jeanstalk	118	T10
2	144		Talking to the giant	112	S6
3	145		Words within words	101	W8
1	150	Mrs Leach and the Leaks	I saw a...	115	T6
2	150		Fred's bread and Doctor Deer	94	W3
3	151		Ea snap	95	W3
1	155	Fact or Fiction?	Fact or fiction?	121	T13
2	156		Noting the facts	127	T19
3	156		Cartoons	110	S5
4	157		Match the meaning	107	W10
5	158		Spelling difficult words	102	W9
1	163	Indexes	Find out where	124	T15
2	164		Make an index	125	T15
3	164		Find the telephone number	123	T15
4	165		Where does it belong?	103	W9
1	167	Book Covers	Cover story	126	T18
2	168		The language of books	104	W9
1	171	Questions	5Ws: who, where, when, what, why?	122	T14
2	171		The question mark challenge	111	S6
3	172		What's in a word?	100	W8
1	176	A Night Out	The school trip	116	T6
2	176		The school trip – how does it end?	119	T10
3	178		Choose a word, make a sentence	96	W4
4	178		It's a match!	105	W9
5	179		Write a dictionary page	106	W9
1	185	Common Suffixes	The fox and the crow	98	W7
2	186		How does it end?	99	W7
1	189	Past and Present	It was only yesterday	114	T3/S3
2	189		In the past	108	S3
3	190		Matching past and present	109	S3
1	195	Take a Letter	Reading detectives	113	T2
2	196		The tortoises' picnic	117	T6

Teachers' notes

p28 MATCHING SOUNDS

Objective
Understand the common spelling patterns for the vowel phonemes oo, ar, oy and ow. (Y2, T1, W3)

Lesson context
This activity is intended to follow work on vowel phonemes and to reinforce children's understanding that the same vowel phoneme may be made using different graphemes.

Setting the homework
Show the children examples of words and sentences like those on the homework sheet and do a few with the class so that they understand how to set about their task.

Differentiation
More able children could be asked to make up further sentences for their parents or helpers to attempt.

Back at school
As a quick assessment of whether all the children have been able to complete this activity, do some more examples on the board and ask children to match the sounds.

MATCH IT!

Objective
Understand the common spelling patterns for the vowel phonemes oo, ar, oy and ow. (Y2, T1, W3)

Lesson context
Use this homework to reinforce work on vowel phonemes.

Setting the homework
Show the children how to play the matching game by using large cards with three matching pairs of words and playing a simple game, with the whole class watching.

Differentiation
You may need to spend a little time with some children reading through the words on the sheet and discussing them. More able children could be asked to add pairs of words to those provided.

Back at school
Play the game with the whole class using a small number of words and discussing the vowel phonemes and their graphemes.

p30 DOWN TOWN

Objective
Understand the common spelling patterns for the vowel phonemes oo, ar, oy and ow. (Y2, T1, W3)

Lesson context
This homework should follow up work on classifying words according to their vowel phonemes.

Setting the homework
Show the children a chart similar to the one on the sheet and ask them where to place words which you've written on cards.

Differentiation
Some children may need to have the text read to them before they take it home. More able children could make use of other texts to find words to add to their charts.

Back at school
Show the children the chart and ask them to contribute further words to it. Talk about the spellings and sounds of the words.

p31 ODD ONE OUT

Objective
Investigate and classify words with the same sounds but different spellings. (Y2, T1, W4)

Lesson context
Use this homework to reinforce work on phonics and to focus attention upon auditory discrimination.

Setting the homework
Show the children examples of sets of words with highlighted graphemes in which one word has a different sound from the others.

Differentiation
More able children could make up further sets of words similar to those on the homework sheet.

Back at school
Ask the children to identify odd words out from sets of words which you have produced on the board. Check that all children are able to hear the vowel phonemes and distinguish between them.

p32 ONE TO TEN

Objective
Investigate words with the same sounds but different spellings. (Y2, T1, W4)

Lesson context
Use this homework to reinforce the idea that words may have different spellings for the same sounds.

Setting the homework
Explain to the children that the poems are simple ones which help people to remember the order of the numbers one to ten. Ask them to look at the rhyming words at the end of each pair of lines.

Differentiation
There are further lines for 'One, two, buckle my shoe', going up to twenty. Some children could be given these to read and be asked to learn spellings of numbers eleven to twenty. Rhymes for these numbers may be limited given that so many end with 'teen'.

Back at school
Conduct a shared writing session in which the whole class helps you to write an alternative version of one of the rhymes. Note the children's awareness of rhymes and of the different ways in which these may sometimes be spelled.

100 LITERACY HOMEWORK ACTIVITIES • YEAR 2 TERM 1

p33 NUMBER RHYMES

Objective
Investigate words with the same sounds but different spellings. (Y2, T1, W4)

Lesson context
This homework should follow a lesson in which children have been exploring rhymes. It should enable them to become increasingly familiar with the spellings of numbers one to ten, but the main objective is to develop an awareness that there are often different spellings for the same sounds.

Setting the homework
Explain to the children that they will be looking for words which rhyme with the numbers one to ten.

Differentiation
The least able children could be given their sheets partially completed.

Back at school
Create a display with the names of the numbers written on an enlarged chart and the class's suggested rhymes written next to them.

p34 WORDS WE USE A LOT

Objective
Read on sight high-frequency words. (Y2, T1, W5)

Lesson context
This homework could follow any lesson in which you have focused upon frequently used words.

Setting the homework
Provide the children with a piece of text appropriate to their reading level and explain that they will be trying to find as many as possible of the words listed on their sheets. For example, give them the story 'Lost on the beach' on page 48.

Differentiation
Provide different pieces of text for children according to their ability levels. More able children could use newspapers or be asked to find their own texts.

Back at school
Invite the children to share some of the sentences they have identified containing high-frequency words. Revise the spelling of these words.

p35 SPELLING GAME

Objective
Spell common words. (Y2, T1, W5/9)

Lesson context
Use this activity to follow up work focusing on frequently used words, for example from the high-frequency list 1 in the NLS *Framework for Teaching*.

Setting the homework
Ensure that children and parents are familiar with the 'Look, say, cover, write, check' approach to learning spellings.

Differentiation
Some children might be asked to use a smaller number of words than on the sheet, while others may be given additional words.

Back at school
As a quick assessment of whether all the children have been able to complete this activity, hold informal spelling quizzes with different ability groups.

p36 SOLOMON GRUNDY

Objective
Learn and spell the days of the week. (Y2, T1, W5/9/10)

Lesson context
This homework should be used to reinforce work on the order and spelling of the days of the week.

Setting the homework
Explain to the children that their homework activity should help them to remember the names of the days of the week and that they should also learn how to spell them.

Differentiation
More able children could be asked to write a simple rhyme with the parents/helpers which would help others to remember the sequence of days of the week.

Back at school
Conduct a simple spelling quiz to check if children are able to spell the names of the days of the week. Help them to remember how to spell Wednesday by teaching them to remember its mispronunciation 'Wed-nes-day'.

p37 MONTHS OF THE YEAR

Objective
Learn the sequence and spellings of the months of the year. (Y2, T1, W5/10)

Lesson context
Use this homework to reinforce work on the months of the year and other high-frequency words.

Setting the homework
Explain to the children that the poem describes what the poet thinks each month of the year brings. Ask them to read the poem at home with their parents/helpers and then practise the order of the months and how to spell them.

Differentiation
Some children might not be asked to learn all of the spellings of the months but could be limited to some of the simpler names such as March, April, May, June and July. More able children could be asked to write their own poems or parts of poems for the months.

Back at school
Hold an informal spelling quiz to see if children are able to spell the names of the months. Discuss some of the similarities or common features of the spellings of some months, ie January and February; and September, October, November and December.

p38 SPELL IT!

Objective
Be able to spell common irregular words. (Y2, T1, W9)

Lesson context
This activity should follow a lesson in which the children have explored some high-frequency words that have irregular spellings.

Setting the homework
Ensure that children and parents are familiar with the 'Look, say, cover, write, check' method of learning spellings.

Differentiation
Children of lower ability should be given fewer words to learn, while those of higher ability might be asked to learn further irregular words.

Back at school
Conduct an informal spelling quiz to ascertain if children have learned the spellings and retained them. You may wish to do this again a few days later to determine whether they are still able to spell the words.

p39 ALPHABETICAL ORDER

Objective
Be able to spell common irregular words and develop an understanding of alphabetical order. (Y2, T1, W9)

Lesson context
Use this activity following class work on common irregular words and/or alphabetical order.

Setting the homework
Spend some time showing children how to use the second and third letters to determine alphabetical order when words have the same beginnings. You could use common irregular words for this activity or you could use names of children in the class.

Differentiation
You may wish to provide more able children with longer lists of words including some in which the first three letters are the same.

Back at school
Check children's ability to spell irregular words by holding an informal spelling quiz. Follow the homework by introducing alphabetical order in indexes and directories. Children will meet these in Term 2.

p40 LABEL YOUR HOME

Objective
Learn new words related to a particular topic: the home. (Y2, T1, W10)

Lesson context
This activity could be linked to a lesson in which the children have been labelling diagrams or it could be linked to one in which they have been learning new words related to the home.

Setting the homework
Ensure that all children know what to do by going over the 'What to do' section on the sheet.

Differentiation
You may wish to provide some children with fewer and simpler words. The most able readers should be encouraged to add further words of their own.

Back at school
As a quick assessment of whether all the children have been able to complete this activity, provide some labels which could relate to items both at home and in school and ask some children to use them in the classroom. Look through all of the labels with the children and ask them to read them aloud.

p41 FIND IT!

Objective
Learn new words related to a particular topic: the home. (Y2, T1, W10)

Lesson context
Link this homework to a lesson in which you have been looking at items in the home and their spellings. Try some sample questions in class to give the children the idea of how to play. For example, write some words relating to items in the classroom and ask questions such as: 'It is white and you can write on the board with it. What is it?'

Setting the homework
Explain to the children that they will need to cut out words from the worksheet and play a game with their parents or helpers.

Differentiation
Some children may need to look at the words with you or with a classroom assistant before taking them home. Others may be invited to add further words at home.

Back at school
As a quick assessment of whether all the children have been able to complete this activity, write the words on the board and play the questions game with them.

p42 AT THE SEASIDE

Objective
Learn new words linked to a particular topic: the seaside. (Y2, T1, W10)

Lesson context
This activity could be linked to a lesson in which holidays have been discussed.

Setting the homework
Explain to the children that they will be learning some words related to being at the seaside. Talk with them about using 'Look, say, cover, write, check' to learn to spell words.

Differentiation
Some children may be asked to play the game with fewer words than others. More able children could be asked to add new words and pictures related to the seaside.

Back at school
As a quick assessment of whether all the children have been able to complete this activity, prepare a set of word cards that have seaside vocabulary. Show these to the children and ask them to read them to you.

p43 CHOOSE THE RIGHT WORD

Objective
Use awareness of grammar and context clues to predict missing words. (Y2, T1, S1)

Lesson context
The homework could be used to follow up work designed to develop semantic and syntactic skills in reading.

Setting the homework
Show the children a few examples of sentences with words missing and ask them to suggest words which would complete them. Talk about using the text before and after a missing word to help determine what the word might be.

Differentiation
Some children could be given the sentences to complete without having a selection of words provided.

Back at school
Try further examples with the whole class or with groups of children to ascertain if they are able to make use of semantic and syntactic clues.

p44 CLEANING YOUR TEETH

Objectives
Develop and reinforce knowledge of directions and instructions; look at words that link sentences. (Y2, T1, S2/T14/16)

Lesson context
This activity may be used to follow up sentence-level work in which the focus has been on words that link sentences. It might also be used to follow up text-level work on instructions and directions.

Setting the homework
Ensure that children understand that link words (such as 'first', 'next', 'after', 'before', 'when' and 'finally') help us to show sequence in texts.

Differentiation
More able children could be asked to change the beginnings of some of the sentences to include words such as 'meanwhile' and 'during'.

Back at school
Check that children have understood the purpose of the linking words by doing some shared writing of instructions or a story.

p45 PUNCTUATE THE PASSAGE

Objective
Read for sense and punctuation. (Y2, T1, S4)

Lesson context
This activity may be used to follow up lessons on the use of commas and full stops.

Setting the homework
Ensure that the children know about the use and purpose of full stops and commas. Read a bit of the passage on the homework sheet, without pausing at all. Ask the children to identify what's wrong. Explain that they should read the passage with their helper and put in the punctuation that will help the reader to read and understand the passage.

Differentiation
Some children may need to work on only a portion of the text, or a simpler text altogether.

Back at school
Display a correctly punctuated copy of the passage and discuss with the children how the punctuation has helped both reading and understanding.

p46 JILL AND JACK

Objective
Revise knowledge about the use of capital letters. (Y2, T1, S5/T1)

Lesson context
This activity should follow lessons in which children have explored the use of capital letters for proper nouns and for the beginnings of sentences or speech.

Setting the homework
Explain that the children have a story to read and that they will need to look closely at the capital letters in the story and decide why each is used.

Differentiation
More able children might be given a more challenging text. Less able children may need simpler text and could be given a copy of a page of their school reading book.

Back at school
Look at an enlarged version of the text with the children and ask them to take turns to explain the reason for each capital letter.

p47 FIND THE CAPITALS

Objective
Revise knowledge about the use of capital letters. (Y2, T1, S5)

Lesson context
This activity should be used as a follow-up to classroom work on capital letters.

Setting the homework
Explain that the children will need to use their reading books and other texts to find capital letters and then will classify them according to the reasons for their usage.

Differentiation
Ensure that children use texts which are appropriate to their reading levels.

Back at school
Make a class chart similar to that on the homework sheet and, using a piece of text currently being used for shared reading, fill in the chart and display it next to the text.

p48 LOST ON THE BEACH

Objective
Understand time and sequential relationships in stories, ie what happened when. (Y2, T1, T4)

Lesson context
This homework would be appropriate for any lesson in which a story has been read and the sequence of events has been discussed with the children.

Setting the homework
Explain that the children are being given the first part of a story. They should read it with their parents or helpers and talk about the order in which events take place. They can then talk about what might happen next in the story.

Differentiation
It should be emphasised that everyone should read the story with their helper but that some children may wish to read it independently as well.

Back at school
Discuss the story with the children. You may wish to use the homework as a starting point for extended writing in which the children complete the story.

p49 WHAT HAPPENED AND WHEN?

Objective
Understand time and sequential relationships in stories. (Y2, T1, T4)

Lesson context
Use this homework to follow up lessons in which children have looked at the structure of stories.

Setting the homework
Explain that children will be using a framework to help them to write a story with their parents or helpers.

Differentiation
Less able children may need help at school with reading words such as 'suddenly' and 'hardly'.

Back at school
Ask the children to read their stories aloud. Discuss the way in which some words and phrases show us that time has moved on in a story.

p50 READING INSTRUCTIONS

Objective
Develop and reinforce the ability to read directions and instructions. (Y2, T1, T13)

Lesson context
This homework may be used as a follow-up to a lesson in which children have explored instructions.

Setting the homework
Talk with the children about paper aeroplanes and ensure that everyone understands what they are.

Differentiation
Less able children may need to become familiarised with some of the vocabulary in the instructions before attempting the homework.

Back at school
Ask the children to bring in their paper aeroplanes, and talk with them about the quality of the instructions.

p51 HOW TO PLAY 'CONCENTRATION'

Objectives
Read and follow simple instructions; develop familiarity with the days of the week (Y2, T1, T13/W5).

Lesson context
This activity could follow any lesson on reading or writing instructions. The words are all related to the days of the week and should, therefore, reinforce children's knowledge of them.

Setting the homework
Explain that the sheet includes instructions for a game and that these should be read with a parent/helper and then followed so that a game may be played.

Differentiation
More able children could have further words related to the calendar, such as months of the year.

Back at school
Discuss the game with the children and talk about the way in which the instructions are set out.

p52 STICK IN THE MUD

Objectives
Be able to read simple instructions; read and recite poems. (Y2, T1, T13/7)

Lesson context
This homework could be used to follow up lessons on instructions and to develop children's abilities to learn and recite simple rhymes.

Setting the homework
Explain that the game featured on the homework sheet needs at least three players and preferably more. Some children might like to get together (with parents' or helpers' permission) and read the instructions and then play the game. Ask the children to find out some of the rhymes their parents used to determine who would go first in a game.

Differentiation
Less able children may need to have the instructions read to them before they take them home or attempt them with their classmates.

Back at school
Ask the children how effective the instructions were and find out if some people played the game in different ways. Ask children about the rhymes their parents used for games and write some of these on the board to model poetry writing for the children.

p53 MAKING A PANCAKE

Objectives
Read simple written instructions; learn new words related to a particular topic. (Y2, T1, T13/W10)

Lesson context
This activity could follow classwork on instructions and/or topic work on food.

Setting the homework
Explain what utensils and ingredients are. If possible, provide some examples of recipes that have items listed separately.

Differentiation
Some children may need to be given help in advance with some of the words which appear in the recipe. This could form part of guided reading in which you work with a group and look at similiar recipes.

Back at school
Talk with the children about utensils and ingredients. Show further examples of recipes and ask them to tell you which items are utensils and which ingredients.

p54 PLAY THE GAME

Objective
Develop and reinforce knowledge of directions and instructions. (Y2, T1, T14)

Lesson context
Any lesson in which instructions have been discussed.

Setting the homework
Explain that children will need a dice to play the game. You may need to loan dice to some children.

Differentiation
Less able children may need to play similar games in school before attempting the homework. More able children could be asked to produce their own similar board games.

Back at school
Play a short game on the board using an enlarged version of the game board or a different version. Note children's abilities to read and follow instructions.

p55 SIMON SAYS!

Objective
Develop and reinforce knowledge of directions and instructions. (Y2, T1, T14)

Lesson context
Use this homework as a follow-up to any lesson on instructions and directions.

Setting the homework
Ensure that children know their left and right.

Differentiation
Less able children may benefit from trying out similar activities in school before attempting the homework. More able children could add further instruction cards to enhance the game.

Back at school
Ask the children to follow simple written instructions as a class or in ability groups. You could do this by writing a series of instructions similar to those in the homework activity on the board and then pointing to them randomly and asking the children to follow them.

p56 WRITING INSTRUCTIONS

Objective
Develop and reinforce knowledge of directions and instructions. (Y2, T1, T15)

Lesson context
Any lesson that has involved exploring instructions and directions could be followed up with this homework.

Setting the homework
Show some examples of instructions which are accompanied by illustrations and some which consist of illustrations alone. Self-assembly furniture packs are a good source.

Differentiation
Less able children could be asked to draw illustrations and limit written instructions to short phrases.

Back at school
Use some of the children's instructions in the classroom and ask others to attempt to follow them and make paper aeroplanes. Discuss the importance of clarity and precision.

p57 WRITE YOUR OWN RECIPE

Objective
Write simple instructions. (Y2, T1, T15)

Lesson context
Any lesson in which the writing of instructions has been taught or practised would be appropriate before the children are given the homework.

Setting the homework
Discuss flow charts with the children and show them some examples.

Differentiation
You may wish to provide some children with copies of the homework sheet on which you have written the first few words of each sentence and provided a small wordbank related to the recipe.

Back at school
Talk with the children about their recipes and discuss the words which are often used to begin sentences in recipes. Show them further examples of recipes.

p58 HIDE AND SEEK

Objective
Be able to write simple instructions for a game.
(Y2, T1, T15/18)

Lesson context
This homework could be one of a series which follows a series of class lessons focusing on instructions.

Setting the homework
Explain that you would like the children to make use of their knowledge of instructions to write their own instructions for a game. You may wish to show them how to write instructions that match illustrations.

Differentiation
Less able children may be asked to limit their instructions to words and phrases rather than complete sentences but, providing they have adequate support at home, they should be encouraged to work with their parents or helpers to write complete sentences.

Back at school
Read some of the children's instructions aloud and ask the children to comment upon them and compare and contrast different versions.

p59 WRITE YOUR OWN INSTRUCTIONS

Objective
Be able to write simple instructions (Y2, T1, T15/18)

Lesson context
This homework should be given when children have become familiar with the style and presentation of instructions and directions.

Setting the homework
Explain that children will need to find instructions at home and that the following may be useful sources: recipe books, magazines, self-assembly models, do-it-yourself books, manuals for electrical goods.

Differentiation
Less able children will probably need parents or helpers to act as scribes when producing instructions.

Back at school
Show examples of the children's instructions and talk about the words which often begin sentences. Write some of them on the board and discuss their meanings.

p60 GETTING TO SCHOOL

Objective
Be able to write simple instructions. (Y2, T1, T15/16/18)

Lesson context
This activity involves children in reading and writing instructions. It should form part of a series of homework assignments on instructions and directions.

Setting the homework
Give the children one day's prior notice of the homework so that they can think about how they get to school and be prepared for the task.

Differentiation
You may wish to provide a simple wordbank to help some children with their instructions. This could be provided for all children, with more extensive vocabulary being given to the most able.

Back at school
Discuss some of the different ways in which children get to school. Compare sentences beginning with each of the words: 'first', 'next', 'now', 'when', 'finally'.

p61 OOH, LOOK AT THAT!

Objective
Revise reading and spelling of words which contain the long vowel phoneme oo as in 'food' and the short vowel phoneme oo as in 'good'. (Y2, T2, W1)

Lesson context
This activity should follow revision work on long vowel sounds. It focuses on the oo grapheme and should reinforce children's appreciation that the grapheme commonly represents either a long phoneme as in 'food' or a short one as in 'book'.

Setting the homework
Talk about words which include oo and discuss their pronunciation. Explain that the children are going to sort oo words according to their vowel sounds.

Differentiation
Some children could be asked to find further oo words in reading books and to add these to their lists.

Back at school
Make a display with an enlarged chart headed 'good' and 'food' and add words from the homework sheet and others which the children have found and which arise in class work.

p62 MIDNIGHT ADVENTURE

Objective
Identify the phoneme or and know some of its common spelling patterns. (Y2, T2, W2)

Lesson context
This homework should follow up work on words which include the phoneme or and should reinforce children's understanding that the phoneme may be made using different graphemes, for example au, our, aw and or.

Setting the homework
Show the children some examples of words which include the phoneme or and discuss some of the different letter combinations commonly used to make the sound.

Differentiation
More able children could be asked to write further sentences that include or words and to create exercises for each other that involve identifying such words.

Back at school
As a quick assessment of whether all the children have been able to complete this activity, provide each child with a word card with an or word on it. Ask the children to say their words and then ask them to get into groups according to the graphemes within their words which create the or sound.

p63 WORDS FOR ALL

Objective
Identify the phonemes er and or. (Y2, T2, W2)

Lesson context
This homework should follow class work on the phonemes er and or in which the common spelling patterns for the phonemes have been discussed.

Setting the homework
Show the children a selection of common words which include er or or phonemes. Ask them to read these aloud and then distinguish between those with er phonemes and those with or phonemes. Explain that they will be doing something similar for their homework.

Differentiation
Less able children may be given fewer words for the game while the most able could be asked to find additional words.

Back at school
Play the phoneme-matching game with the whole class by giving everyone a word card and asking each child in turn to show the word on their card and say it aloud. Then ask individual children to take turns to ask pairs of children to show their cards. They can be given a point if they choose a pair in which each child has a word with the same phoneme.

p64 CHARLOTTE, CHARLES AND CHLOE

Objective
Read and spell words containing the digraph ch. (Y2, T2, W3)

Lesson context
This homework should follow a lesson or series of lessons which focus on the digraph ch. It is designed to illustrate both the most common pronunciation of ch and other quite common pronunciations.

Setting the homework
Explain to the children that they will be identifying words which include the digraph ch and then sorting them into different categories according to the way in which ch is sounded in each word. You may wish to practise identifying and categorising such words in school before setting the homework – for example, check that the children understand that 'Christmas' sounds like 'Chloe' because of the hard c sound at the beginning of the word.

Differentiation
More able children could be asked to do the homework using other more challenging texts.

Back at school
As a quick assessment of whether all the children have been able to complete this activity, provide an enlarged version of the sentences and ask them to identify and categorise the ch words.

p65 CHEF'S CHOCOLATE

Objective
Read and spell words containing the digraph *ch*.
(Y2, T2, W3)

Lesson context
This homework should follow a lesson or series of lessons which focus on the digraph *ch*. It is designed to illustrate both the most common pronunciation of *ch* and other quite common pronunciations.

Setting the homework
Explain to the children that they will be asked to look at a collection of words and then sort them according to the sound which *ch* makes in each. They should be encouraged to find further *ch* words and sort these too.

Differentiation
Some children might be given a more limited selection of words or could have some of the words categorised for them on an amended version of the homework sheet.

Back at school
Play a matching game with the whole class. Give each child a card with a *ch* word printed on it and ask the children to take turns to stand up and show and say their words. All of the children who have a word with a similar *ch* sound should hold up their cards so that you may check if they have understood the different pronunciations.

p66 WHAT A COLLECTION!

Objective
Read and spell words containing the digraphs *wh* and *ph*.
(Y2, T2, W3)

Lesson context
This homework should follow work on words which include *wh* and *ph*.

Setting the homework
Talk with the children about words which include *ph* and *wh* and discuss the sounds made by the digraphs. Both digraphs produce quite consistent sounds in English but there are exceptions for *ph*, notably the name 'Stephen' in which *ph* represents a *v* rather than an *f* sound.

Differentiation
You may wish to provide simple texts for less able readers rather than asking them to find words in their reading books. More able children could be asked to use dictionaries to find further examples of *wh* and *ph* words.

Back at school
Make a display of examples of *wh* and *ph* words and add those the children have discovered.

p67 TIME TO RHYME

Objective
Read and spell words containing the digraphs *wh* and *ph* and reinforce understanding of rhyme. (Y2, T2, W3)

Lesson context
This homework focuses both on *wh* and *ph* words and on rhyme so children will need to be aware of each before attempting it.

Setting the homework
Talk with the children about rhyme and then relate this directly to words which include *wh* and/or *ph*. Ask them to match other words with similar rimes to the *wh* and *ph* words.

Differentiation
Some children may need to be given fewer and simpler words to work on. These might be limited to common *wh* words which appear in the National Literacy Strategy high-frequency word list 1.

Back at school
Make an enlarged version of the chart from the homework sheet and incorporate the words from the sheet which rhyme and others suggested by the children. The chart could be added to over a period of weeks, as new words arise in lessons.

p68 WORD SUMS

Objective
Split familiar compound words into their component parts.
(Y2, T2, W4)

Lesson context
This homework should follow up work on compound words in which children have looked at the words that are combined to produce common compound words.

Setting the homework
Explain to the children that they will be given a selection of compound words and be asked to split them into the words which go together to form them.

Differentiation
More able children could be provided with additional compound words and be asked to find others in their reading books and other texts.

Back at school
As a quick assessment of whether all the children have been able to complete this activity, write a series of compound words on the board and ask the class to help you to divide them into their constituent parts.

p69 MAKING COMPOUND WORDS

Objective
Build compound words using component parts.
(Y2, T2, W4)

Lesson context
This homework complements work on splitting compound words by requiring children to build compound words.

Setting the homework
Provide a few examples of words that could be combined to make compound words and ask the class to suggest some possible combinations. Encourage the use of simple dictionaries to check the words that are produced.

Differentiation
Children may be provided with more or fewer words according to their ability levels.

Back at school
As a quick assessment of whether all the children have understood this activity, write on the board some words that could be used to make compound words. Ask the children to suggest pairs of words that could be joined to create compounds. You could divide the class into two teams and let each team take turns to come up with a word.

p70 FIND THE COMPOUND WORDS

Objective
Split familiar compound words into their component parts.
(Y2, T2, W4)

Lesson context
This activity involves children in finding compound words in a piece of text and then splitting the words into their component parts. It should follow a series of lessons that focus on compound words.

Setting the homework
Explain to the children that the passage they have been given includes several compound words. You may wish to tell them exactly how many (there are 13 different words – the word 'playground' is repeated). Show them some examples of compound words and ask them to divide the words into their constituent parts.

Differentiation
You may wish to underline some of the compound words to help the less able. More able children could be given a more extensive piece of text to work on.

Back at school
Look at an enlarged version of the text with the children and ask them to identify and then split the compound words. Go on to provide further examples and ask them to do the same with those words.

p71 HOW MANY SYLLABLES?

Objective
Discriminate, orally, syllables in multisyllabic words and note syllable boundaries in speech and writing. (Y2, T2, W5)

Lesson context
The homework should be used to reinforce work done on syllables in a literacy lesson or in music.

Setting the homework
Practise with the children clapping syllables in familiar words and in their names. Explain that they are going to find words with different numbers of syllables.

Differentiation
Some children could be asked to find only one-, two- and three-syllable words, while others could be challenged to find words with five or more syllables.

Back at school
As a quick assessment of whether all the children have been able to complete this activity, ask individuals to clap their names and those of others.

p72 MATCHING SYLLABLES

Objective
Discriminate, orally, syllables in multisyllabic words and note syllable boundaries in speech and writing. (Y2, T2, W5)

Lesson context
The homework provides a game which follows up work on syllables. It also offers an opportunity to revise work on instructions.

Setting the homework
Explain to the children that they will be playing a matching game based on syllables. You may wish to try the game with the whole class with a limited number of words.

Differentiation
The number and complexity of the words may be varied according to the ability levels of the children. You may wish to provide prepared sets of words for some.

Back at school
As a quick assessment of whether all the children have been able to complete this activity, write a series of words with one, two, three or four syllables on the board and ask the children to help you to sort them according to their numbers of syllables.

p73 THE SECRET GARDEN IN THE CITY

Objective
Read on sight high-frequency words. (Y2, T2, W6)

Lesson context
The homework could be used to follow up spelling work on high-frequency words.

Setting the homework
Explain that the text is surrounded by common words and that the children need to draw a line from the words at the top and the bottom to the same words in the text.

Differentiation
Less able children may be given fewer high-frequency words to find, while the most able might be asked to find the words in a more complex piece of text.

Back at school
Hold an informal spelling quiz based upon the high-frequency words and note children's abilities to spell them accurately.

p74 OPPOSITES

Objective
Understand the use of antonyms and discuss differences of meaning. (Y2, T2, W11/8)

Lesson context
This activity should follow work on antonyms in class and should reinforce children's awareness of their spellings and meanings.

Setting the homework
Explain that there are two lists on the homework sheet and that the children need to draw lines to link the words that are antonyms of each other. Provide an example on the board.

Differentiation
More able children could be asked to produce further lists of antonyms for each other to attempt at school.

Back at school
Make a list on the board of some of the additional antonyms which children found and ask the class to match the pairs. Talk about spellings and about any prefixes that are used to create antonyms.

p75 FIND THE OPPOSITE

Objective
Understand the use of antonyms and discuss differences of meaning. (Y2, T2, W11/8)

Lesson context
This activity develops children's understanding of antonyms and their meanings. It should be used to follow up class work on prefixes.

Setting the homework
Explain that the worksheet has a list of words, each of which has at least one antonym. Provide a few examples on the board and ask children to consider possible antonyms. Talk about the use of prefixes such as *un-* and *dis-* which may be used to create some antonyms.

Differentiation
More able children could be asked to use dictionaries to find examples of words that begin with *un-* and *dis-* and to write some of them in a list. You will need to talk about other words which begin with *un-* and *dis-* in which *un-* and *dis-* are not prefixes for antonyms (eg 'united', 'university', 'dish', 'disgust').

Back at school
Look at some of the examples of antonyms that the children have found and focus on those which have the prefixes *un-* or *dis-*. Provide further examples and see if the children have understood how to add a prefix to make a negative.

p76 STOP THROWING PAINT!

Objective
Use awareness of grammar to predict from a text appropriate missing words. (Y2, T2, S1)

Lesson context
This activity should follow up work done on speech marks and work done on verbs that focuses on the way verbs can be used to show how speech is spoken.

Setting the homework
Explain to the children that they will be reading a piece of dialogue and that they will need to read it carefully to decide how each speaker might have said the words that are spoken.

Differentiation
Read the dialogue with children who may need to become familiar with the vocabulary before taking the text home. Some children may need to be given simpler text to work on.

Back at school
Talk about the verbs that the children ascribed to each speaker and then look at further examples of such verbs in texts that are familiar to the children.

p77 PAINTING

Objective
Use awareness of grammar to predict from a text appropriate missing words. (Y2, T2, S1)

Lesson context
This activity may follow up cloze work in class.

Setting the homework
Talk about the ways in which we can read beyond missing or unfamiliar words to try to understand what they are or what they mean. Explain to the children that they have been given a piece of writing with some words missing and that their task is to fill in the spaces.

Differentiation
More able children may be given the text without a selection of words to use and be asked to work out their own.

Back at school
Make an enlarged version of the text and read it with the children and then use their suggestions to complete it. Look for evidence that they are able to use grammatical sense to do this and that they can justify their choices when these differ from those of others.

p78 WHO SAID THAT?

Objective
Use verb tenses with increasing accuracy in writing. (Y2, T2, S5)

Lesson context
This activity could follow work on speech marks or on character sketches. It requires children to use the correct tense for verbs that denote the way in which speech is spoken.

Setting the homework
Show children some examples from the current class story book of verbs which accompany speech and talk about the way they tend to be written in the past tense. Explain that the children will be looking at similar verbs and will need to write them in the correct tense.

Differentiation
Ask more able children to use their reading books to find other examples of verbs used to describe speech.

Back at school
Look at further examples of verbs and, with the children's help, write these in both the present and past tenses.

p79 WHAT'S BLACK AND WHITE AND READ ALL OVER?

Objective
Identify speech marks in reading and understand their purpose. (Y2, T2, S6)

Lesson context
This homework should follow work on identifying speech marks. It requires children to identify speakers and to read aloud.

Setting the homework
Remind children of the purpose of speech marks and show them an example of dialogue. Read this with the class, perhaps asking half of them to read the words of one character and the other half those of another. Emphasise that it is only the words within the speech marks that should be spoken and ask one child to read all of the words that are not speech.

Differentiation
Any children whom you feel may find the text difficult could be provided with simpler dialogue or could be asked to use a page from their reading books as the basis for the activity.

Back at school
As a quick assessment of whether all the children have been able to complete this activity, look at an enlarged example of dialogue and ask them to read only the spoken words aloud. You could follow this up further in group reading, with children taking turns to read by being assigned characters whose speech they should read.

p80 MAKE A SPEECH!

Objective
Understand the purpose of speech marks and use them in shared writing. (Y2, T2, S6)

Lesson context
This activity provides an opportunity for children to use speech marks with the help of an adult. It should follow lessons in which children have taken part in shared writing using speech marks.

Setting the homework
Explain that the pictures on the worksheet tell a story and that the children will be writing a dialogue to go with them.

Differentiation
Some children may be asked to write only the spoken words as in a cartoon. They could then be helped in school to use speech marks to record the dialogue.

Back at school
Look with the class at some examples of dialogue written by the children and talk about the words that are spoken and the positioning of the speech marks. Check that the children have understood that speech marks go around spoken words only.

p81 CHANGING SENTENCES

Objective
Secure the use of simple sentences and discuss differences in meaning of antonyms. (Y2, T2, S9/W11)

Lesson context
This activity develops children's appreciation of antonyms and requires them to use antonyms in the context of sentences. It should follow up work on antonyms that has focused on verbs.

Setting the homework
Show the children some examples of sentences in which changing one or more words to their antonym would change the meaning. Explain that sometimes more than one word may be changed.

Differentiation
For less able children, underline words that should be changed.

Back at school
Look at some of the children's sentences and compare any different versions.

p82 DESCRIPTIONS

Objective
Write simple descriptions and secure the use of simple sentences in own writing. (Y2, T2, S9/T6)

Lesson context
This activity involves using nouns and adjectives to create sentences that describe. It should form part of a series of lessons on sentence construction and writing character profiles.

Setting the homework
Write a few adjectives and a few nouns on the board and ask the children to choose words from each list and make up sentences. Explain that the homework will give them the opportunity to make up sentences of their own.

Differentiation
More able children could go on to select their own adjectives and nouns and write further, more extensive descriptions.

Back at school
Look with the class at some examples of descriptive sentences produced by the children. Talk about the parts of speech and the use of capital letters and punctuation.

p83 ADJECTIVES FOR ANDREW

Objective
Write simple descriptions and secure the use of simple sentences in own writing. (Y2, T2, S9/T6)

Lesson context
This homework involves reading a description of a character and identifying adjectives. It should follow similar work in class.

Setting the homework
Explain that the homework sheet has a description of a boy and that the children will be answering some questions about him. Show the children a sample sentence and ask them to identify adjectives.

Differentiation
Less able children could be given more simple text, perhaps taken from their reading books, while the more able may be provided with more challenging character descriptions.

Back at school
Ask the children to identify adjectives in sentences you have written on the board and check that they understand the term adjective.

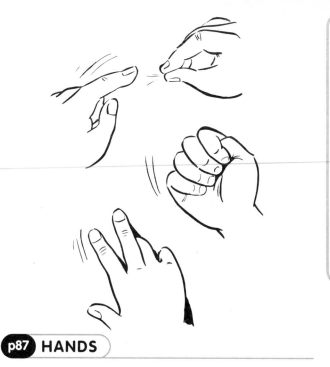

p84 TWO DIFFERENT PEOPLE?

Objective
Secure the use of simple sentences and discuss differences in meaning of antonyms. (Y2, T2, S9/W11/T14)

Lesson context
This activity should follow up work on antonyms and/or on character profiles. It is designed to reinforce this work and provide an opportunity for children to demonstrate a growing understanding of antonyms.

Setting the homework
Explain that we need to choose our words carefully if we are to provide accurate descriptions of people. Show some examples of descriptions of people that could be changed dramatically if one or two words were altered.

Differentiation
Very able children could be asked to write their own contrasting character profiles.

Back at school
Enlarge or copy out some examples of children's work and discuss the antonyms they have used. If any children have written their own profiles, look at these with the class and discuss the antonyms that have been used.

p85 MISSING MOUSE

Objective
Predict story endings. (Y2, T2, T4)

Lesson context
This homework should follow lessons in which children have taken part in shared reading of unfinished stories and have discussed or written endings.

Setting the homework
Read the story with the children and explain that they will be writing an ending for it. You may wish to discuss possibilities in order to give them some ideas, but emphasise that they should work out their own endings.

Differentiation
Parents of less able children could be encouraged to act as scribes for their children. Alternatively, the children may be asked to read with their parents and then make notes which can be turned into a story at school with the help of an adult or as a whole-class shared writing activity.

p86 CHARACTER SKETCHES

Objective
Identify and describe characters. (Y2, T2, T6/14)

Lesson context
This homework should follow lessons on character description.

Setting the homework
Explain that the sheet has descriptions of characters and pictures of them but that the pictures and descriptions need to be sorted out so that they match. Talk about the use of adjectives to describe characters and encourage the children to use them when they are writing their own character sketches.

Differentiation
More able children may be asked to write more character sketches and should be encouraged to look for descriptions in story books.

Back at school
Ask the children to read aloud some of their character sketches. Write some of the adjectives they use on the board and discuss their meanings and spellings.

p87 HANDS

Objective
Read poems aloud and discuss using appropriate terms. (Y2, T2, T8/10/11)

Lesson context
Use this homework to follow up work on poetry. In the poem 'Hands' there are many examples of verbs ending with -ing. Talk about such words in lessons before giving the homework.

Setting the homework
Read the poem aloud to the children and then with them. Ask them to look, in particular, at the verbs that end with -ing. Explain that they will be reading the poem at home and then writing one of their own.

Differentiation
Less able children who may experience difficulty in writing poems could produce list poems in which only one word (a verb) is used on each of six lines following the word 'Hands'.

Back at school
Ask the children to read aloud their poems, and write some of the verbs they have used on the board and discuss their spellings.

p88 WINTER MORNING

Objective
Discuss poems using appropriate terms. (Y2, T2, T11)

Lesson context
This homework should follow a lesson in which children have taken part in shared reading of poems and have discussed poetry using terms such as rhyme, poet and describe.

Setting the homework
Explain to the children that they will be given a poem to read and that there are some questions which they will need to answer.

Differentiation
More able children may be asked to look at other poems and make up questions to go with them.

Back at school
Look at the poem with the whole class and answer the questions together. Talk about other poems that the children know and ask them to answer similar questions. If some children looked at other poems for their homework, make use of these.

p89 BOOKS ARE GREAT!

Objective
Identify and discuss patterns of rhyme. (Y2, T2, T11)

Lesson context
This lesson should follow up class work on poetry that includes exploring and discussing rhymes.

Setting the homework
Explain that the poem contains many rhymes and that, when the children have read it, they will be looking for pairs of rhyming words. Discuss the rhyming of 'in' and 'been', which depends upon 'been' being pronounced 'bin'.

Differentiation
Ask some of the most able children to look at other poems and songs to find further examples of rhymes that depend upon words being pronounced in a slightly unconventional way.

Back at school
Read the poem with the class and discuss the rhymes. Ask if anyone has discovered any other rhymes. Talk about them and discuss spellings.

p90 NOSES

Objective
Read a poem aloud and identify rhymes. (Y2, T2, T11/8)

Lesson context
This homework should follow class work on poetry that focuses in particular on reading aloud and rhyme.

Setting the homework
Explain that the children will be reading a poem and looking for rhyming words in it. You may wish to read the poem to the class first.

Differentiation
You may wish to ask parents and helpers of less able children to read the poem aloud, encouraging the children to join in where they are able.

Back at school
Read the poem with the children and ask them to identify the rhyming words. Write these on the board and ask the class to suggest further words that would rhyme with them. Talk about the different spelling patterns that can be used to create the same sounds.

p91 WRITE A POEM

Objective
Use structures from poems as a basis for writing. (Y2, T2, T15)

Lesson context
This homework should follow lessons in which children have read simple poems aloud and taken part in shared writing of poetry.

Setting the homework
Explain that the sheet has a partially written poem which the children are going to complete. Tell them that they may use their own ideas to do this.

Differentiation
Less able children may need to be given a more complete version of the poem, while the more able may be asked to write additional verses.

Back at school
Ask some children to read their poems aloud and talk about the words they have used. Look for evidence that they are able to make their poems scan and can read them aloud with expression.

p92 SHOPPING AT THE SUPERMARKET

Objective
Produce a simple flow chart that explains a process. (Y2, T2, T21)

Lesson context
This homework should follow class work on flow charts.

Setting the homework
Explain that the children will be given a sheet with boxes in which different stages of shopping at the supermarket are described. They will then have to read them carefully and place them in the correct order. If any children are unfamiliar with supermarkets, spend time discussing supermarkets and the ways in which they differ from small shops.

Differentiation
More able children could be asked to produce their own flow charts for shopping.

Back at school
Ask the children to take turns to show their versions of the flow chart to the rest of the class. Make an enlarged flow chart for another process.

p93 MAKE YOUR OWN FLOW CHART

Objective
Produce a simple flow chart that explains a process. (Y2, T2, T21)

Lesson context
This homework should reinforce children's understanding of flow charts.

Setting the homework
Explain that the homework sheet has an example of a flow chart and that you would like the children to choose another process and create their own flow charts.

Differentiation
Children could be encouraged to include more or fewer stages in their processes according to ability. The least able could confine their writing to simple words and phrases accompanied by sketches.

Back at school
Look at the children's flow charts with the whole class and discuss them. Choose some good examples and enlarge them so that everyone may look at them together. Make a further flow chart with the whole class to check on the children's understanding.

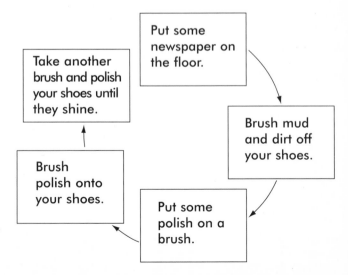

p94 FRED'S BREAD AND DOCTOR DEER

Objective
Discriminate, spell and read the phonemes *ear* and *ea*. (Y2, T3, W3)

Lesson context
This homework is intended to follow a lesson examining the long and short e sounds.

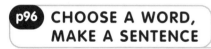

Setting the homework
Explain to the children that they need to read these two funny poems aloud and listen carefully for the different sounds made by *ea* in words. If necessary, model a couple of examples.

Differentiation
More able children who can discriminate, spell and read the phonemes *ear* and *ea* could be encouraged to find more examples of words containing these phonemes.

Back at school
Display in sets the words that share the same sound and spelling.

p95 EA SNAP

Objective
Discriminate, spell and read the phonemes *ear* and *ea*. (Y2, T3, W3)

Lesson context
Use this lesson to follow up work focusing on the long and short e sounds.

Setting the homework
Explain to the children that they will be making and playing a game of 'Snap', looking for the words that have the same *ea* sound. Ensure they know the rules of the game.

Back at school
Ask groups of children to play the game, for reinforcement.

p96 CHOOSE A WORD, MAKE A SENTENCE

Objective
Spell high-frequency words. (Y2, T3, W4)

Lesson context
This homework should follow any word-level work involving putting high-frequency words into the context of a sentence, to ensure understanding of the meaning and to reinforce learning to spell the words.

Setting the homework
Explain to the children that they will need to select words from the list to use in writing sentences. You may like to model one example; you could choose 'about', which is used as the example on the sheet. Ask various children to give sentences using 'about'.

Differentiation
For less able children, you may like to restrict the number of words from which to select. More able children could be encouraged to choose more than four words to use in sentences.

Back at school
Display examples of sentences next to a wordbank of high-frequency words.

p97 SOUNDS OF THE CITY

Objective
Reinforce work from previous terms on different spellings of the same phoneme. (Y2, T3, W1)

Lesson context
This homework should follow a lesson that has included investigating different spellings of the same phoneme, specifically the sound s represented by the graphemes *s*, *se*, *ss*, *c* and *ce*.

Setting the homework
Explain to the children that they will be reading a poem to see which words rhyme and to explore the different spellings of the sound s.

Differentiation
Some children's phonological awareness may not be sufficiently developed to enable them to investigate a range of graphemes for the same phoneme. It may be preferable to focus on a limited number of graphemes, such as only *s* and *ss*.

Back at school
Read the poem with the class and, using an enlarged copy, ask different children to highlight the letters making the sound s.

p98 THE FOX AND THE CROW

Objective
Identify words with common suffixes: *-ed*, *-ly*, *-ful*. (Y2, T3, W7)

Lesson context
This activity could be linked to any word-level work identifying common suffixes.

Setting the homework
Explain to the children that they will need to read the story carefully and then find all the words ending in *-ed*, *-ly* and *-ful*. You might talk about one or two examples, eg 'beautiful', 'talked', 'sadly'.

Differentiation
Ensure that less able children have experienced looking for specific words or word endings.

Back at school
You may like to read the story with the class and ask different children to find words with specific endings.

p99 HOW DOES IT END?

Objective
Match root words to common suffixes: *-ed*, *-ly*, *-ful*. (Y2, T3, W7)

Lesson context
This homework should be used to follow word-level work identifying common suffixes.

Setting the homework
Explain to the children that they will need to cut out the words and word endings and then try and put them together to make proper words. Provide a few examples, eg 'help' + *ful*, 'usual' + *ly*. You may like to explain at this point that for words that already end in e, we drop the e when adding *-ed*, eg 'hate' becomes 'hated'.

Differentiation
This will be largely by outcome, with less able children probably only being able to find more common words.

Back at school
Have sets of the cards made up and laminated for use in school, so that the children can show you the words they made. You could also make up one enlarged set to display and use with the whole class.

p100 WHAT'S IN A WORD?

Objective
Spell common irregular words: words beginning with *wh-*. (Y2, T3, W8)

Lesson context
This homework should follow any lesson that has involved looking closely at words and finding words within them, or a lesson focusing on posing questions.

Setting the homework
Explain to the children that they will be looking for words hidden inside the question words 'what', 'when' and 'where'. If possible, model finding words within a word using an example not on the sheet.

Differentiation
This will largely be by outcome, according to the number of words children find.

Back at school
Display the number of words found in the classroom.

p101 WORDS WITHIN WORDS

Objective
Spell unfamiliar words. (Y2, T3, W8)

Lesson context
This homework is intended to follow any lesson that has involved looking closely at words and finding words or letter patterns within them.

Setting the homework
Explain to the children that they need to find words hidden inside the longer words. If possible, work through one example with the class.

Differentiation
This will largely be by outcome, according to the number of words children find.

Back at school
Display the number of words found, possibly by the classroom door so that parents and helpers can see the results!

p102 SPELLING DIFFICULT WORDS

Objective
Spell new words. (Y2, T3, W9)

Lesson context
Use this homework to follow up spelling activities in word-level work that look at ways of learning irregular words, eg splitting the words into syllables.

Setting the homework
Explain to the children that they will be using the 'Look, say, cover, write, check' method to learn to spell new words.

Differentiation
You may wish to restrict the number of words for less able children.

Back at school
Include these words in a routine spelling test to assess whether the children have successfully learned the spellings.

p103 WHERE DOES IT BELONG?

Objective
Build a collection of words by matching words to the correct alphabetical section. (Y2, T3, W9)

Lesson context
This activity should follow on from a lesson that has involved sorting information into categories and then putting the categories in correct alphabetical order.

Setting the homework
Discuss catalogues with the children and tell them that they will be selecting words from the lists at the top of the sheet to write in the correct sections, remembering to use alphabetical order. You may need to explain the word 'accessories'.

Back at school
The information on the completed homework sheets could form part of a class activity in which the children put together a catalogue comprising pages that they have made themselves.

p104 THE LANGUAGE OF BOOKS

Objective
Define words linked to particular topics. (Y2, T3, W9)

Lesson context
This activity should follow up a shared reading session in which the children have been looking closely at book covers.

Setting the homework
Explain to the children that they will need to look closely at the picture of the book cover and the labels around it. They will then need to write what each of the words means. You might like to provide one example, such as 'illustrator – the person who draws the illustrations or pictures in the book'.

Differentiation
You could extend this activity for more able children by asking them to look at a range of books at home or in the local library and compile a list of titles, authors, illustrators and so on.

Back at school
Prepare some large cards with the terminology title, illustrator, author, publisher, blurb, bar code and price, and ask the children to help label a big book for display in the classroom.

p105 IT'S A MATCH!

Objective
Match definitions to words. (Y2, T3, W9)

Lesson context
This activity could follow any lesson that has involved defining unfamiliar vocabulary.

Setting the homework
Explain to the children that they will be making cards for a game to play with a helper. The game is a pairs game in which they have to match words to their meanings. The vocabulary included on the sheet is the same as that on the next sheet (page 106) and can be found in context in the story 'The school trip' (page 116). The three sheets, along with the sheet on page 119, could be used as a homework sequence.

Differentiation
You may like to include simpler words and definitions for less able children.

Back at school
Ask groups of children to play the game as an independent activity during a literacy lesson.

p106 WRITE A DICTIONARY PAGE

Objective
Write definitions of words. (Y2, T3, W9)

Lesson context
This activity would follow on well from work using dictionaries and reading definitions. The vocabulary included on the sheet is the same as that on the previous sheet (page 105) and can be found in context in the story 'The school trip' (page 116). The three sheets, and the sheet on page 119, could be used as a homework sequence.

Setting the homework
Explain to the children that the words and definitions are at the top of the page and that they need to write the words and the corresponding meanings in the grid. Remind them to make sure that they put the words in alphabetical order.

Differentiation
Less able children could be encouraged to match the words and definitions before completing this homework. Or parents and helpers could be very well briefed.

Back at school
Talk about the words and correct definitions. You could follow this up by making a class dictionary.

p107 MATCH THE MEANING

Objective
Find synonyms for words. (Y2, T3, W10)

Lesson context
This homework could be used to follow up a lesson that has involved investigating synonyms.

Setting the homework
Explain to the children that they will be matching the words to the meanings on the sheet. They can refer to a dictionary if they wish.

Differentiation
Less able children could be provided with simpler words, or the number of words could be limited.

Back at school
Ask different children to share examples of synonyms. Alternatively, if you write some of the words on cards, together with synonyms, you could ask the children to hold up the cards and find a partner who has a word with the same meaning.

p108 IN THE PAST

Objective
Use the past tense consistently for narration. (Y2, T3, S3)

Lesson context
This activity provides an opportunity for children to change sentences written in the present tense to the past tense. It should follow up work that has involved shared writing using the past tense.

Setting the homework
Explain to the children that they will need to rewrite sentences that are in the present tense (happening now) into the past tense (happened before). You may like to model the example given on the sheet.

Differentiation
Less able children may be encouraged to say their sentences aloud, preceding each sentence with 'Yesterday...'.

Back at school
Discuss examples of sentences in the past tense.

p109 MATCHING PAST AND PRESENT

Objective
Match verbs in the present and past tense. (Y2, T3, S3)

Lesson context
This activity could follow up a lesson that has involved shared writing using the past tense, in particular examining irregular examples of the past tense, eg 'dig' and 'dug'.

Setting the homework
Explain to the children that they will need to match the verbs (action words) in the present tense (happening now) with the corresponding ones in the past tense (happened before). You may like to model the example given on the sheet.

Differentiation
Less able children may be encouraged to put the words into sentences, saying their sentences aloud and preceding each appropriately with 'Today...' and 'Yesterday...'. Additionally, you may wish to limit the number of words for less able children.

Back at school
Display examples of words in the past tense and discuss them. For instance, you could make use of a puppet who keeps getting the words in the past tense wrong and the children have to correct him (such as 'I feeled ill', 'I runned fast' and so on).

 **CARTOONS**

Objective
Identify capital letters for proper nouns. (Y2, T3, S5)

Lesson context
Use this homework to follow any lesson which has involved examining the use of capital letters for proper nouns.

Setting the homework
Explain to the children that they will be reading a non-fiction extract about cartoons and that they will need to search carefully for capital letters for names or places or things. They should then write a list of those they find.

Differentiation
Less able children may need support in reading the text. Make sure they understand that a proper noun is the name of a specific person, place or thing. Their own name and the place in which they live could be given as examples.

Back at school
Discuss which words had capital letters and why.

p111 THE QUESTION MARK CHALLENGE

Objective
Punctuate questions correctly. (Y2, T3, S6)

Lesson context
This activity should be used to follow up a lesson that has focused on punctuating questions.

Setting the homework
Explain to the children that they will be reading some text in which the question marks have been taken out. There are many questions in the story, so there are many question marks missing. Can they find them all and put them in?

Differentiation
Less able children may need help in reading the text. They could try sharing the reading with their helper, each taking a role.

Back at school
Enlarge a copy of the story for children to punctuate.

p112 TALKING TO THE GIANT

Objective
Use question marks and exclamation marks correctly. (Y2, T3, S6)

Lesson context
This homework should be used after class work involving punctuating sentences with question marks and exclamation marks. It could follow on from reading the story of Jack and the Beanstalk.

Setting the homework
Explain to the children that they need to add question marks and exclamation marks to the speech bubbles from the story of Jack and the Beanstalk. They will also need to add full stops.

Differentiation
Less able children may need helpers to read the speech with correct intonation to help them decide what punctuation to use.

Back at school
Discuss the punctuation required for these examples. You could enlarge the speech bubbles to form part of a display on Jack and the Beanstalk.

p113 READING DETECTIVES

Objective
Read unfamiliar words by using context cues. (Y2, T3, T2)

Lesson context
This homework should follow up a lesson which has involved modelling the use of context cues during shared reading, for example by masking the word and then reading on to the end of the sentence to try and discover what the word is. Note that the same story is used for the sheet on page 117 and, therefore, these two sheets could form a homework sequence.

Setting the homework
Explain to the children that they will be reading a funny story. Tell them that it contains some words which they may not have read before, so they will need to be detectives and work out the meaning of those words by reading the sentences around each word to help them.

Differentiation
Less able children could be provided with a limited number of words. It would also be helpful if they asked a parent or helper to read the story first to them.

Back at school
Read the story, which you have enlarged, with the class, and talk about some of the less familiar words. If there is time, talk about the humour in the story.

p114 IT WAS ONLY YESTERDAY

Objective
Retell a story in the past tense. (Y2, T3, T3/S3)

Lesson context
This homework can be used once children have experienced telling a story and keeping it consistently in the past tense. A range of experiences of shared reading examining how stories are told in the past tense and then changing verbs from the past to the present, and vice versa, is a prerequisite.

Setting the homework
Explain to the children that they will be reading a story and then retelling the story to a parent or helper, making sure it is in the past, as if the story happened yesterday.

Back at school
Choose one or two children who are willing to tell the story as if it happened yesterday, to the whole class. You may in addition like to ask some children to record their stories onto tape.

p115 I SAW A...

Objective
Read and respond imaginatively to poems. (Y2, T3, T6)

Lesson context
This homework involves reading a poem that requires an imaginative response to find the meaning of what has been said. It should follow any similar work that has been done in class.

Setting the homework
Ask the children to read the poem carefully, and explain that the lines of the poem have become muddled. You might show how by moving half of each line down you get a poem that makes sense, but the weird effect of the muddled lines make an interesting poem. The poem should read:

I saw a beach as in a dream,
I saw a ring that glittered and gleamed,
I saw a pea stuck on a beard,
I saw a head that looked weird,
I saw a pipe made of lead,
I saw a woman spreading butter on bread,
I saw a thread reach up to the sky,
I saw all these things and I wondered why.

Children will need to answer the questions on the poem when they have unmuddled it.

Back at school
Read the poem, and rewrite it on the board with the lines moved. Ask the children to talk about the answers to the questions.

p116 THE SCHOOL TRIP

Objective
Respond to questions on a text that has been read. (Y2, T3, T6)

Lesson context
This activity should follow on from any lesson that has involved close reading of a text and answering questions.

Setting the homework
Ask the children to read the extract carefully with their parent or helper and then write answers to the questions, remembering to write in full sentences. The activity is linked to sheets on pages 105, 106 and 119. The four sheets could be used as a homework sequence.

Back at school
Read the story together and ask different children to provide answers to the questions.

p117 THE TORTOISES' PICNIC

Objective
Respond to literal and non-literal questions on a text. (Y2, T3, T6)

Lesson context
This homework could be used to follow up any lesson in which children have had the experience of answering a range of questions on a text. Note that the same story is used for the sheet on page 113 and, therefore, these two sheets could form a homework sequence.

Setting the homework
Ask the children to read the story with their parents or helpers and then answer the questions.

Back at school
Read the story with the class and ask one or two children to share their answers to the questions.

p118 SACK AND THE JEANSTALK

Objective
Write sentences to fit a known story. (Y2, T3, T10)

Lesson context
This homework could follow on from reading the story of Jack and the Beanstalk and possibly also the complete story of 'Sack and the Jeanstalk' contained in *Scholastic Literacy Centre, Fiction Green Set: Teachers' Resources* (Scholastic Ltd).

Setting the homework
Explain to the children that they will be reading an extract from a funny version of Jack and the Beanstalk. They will need to find which words are wrong, eg 'Once upon a line...', and underline all those words. Then they should look carefully at the pictures of the beginning, middle and end of the correct story, and write sentences to fit each picture.

Back at school
Discuss the wrong words that the children have identified in 'Sack and the Jeanstalk', then invite them to read out their sentences relating to the original story. Display enlarged copies of the pictures on the homework sheet together with the sentences that the children have written.

p119 THE SCHOOL TRIP – HOW DOES IT END?

Objective
Write an ending to a story. (Y2, T3, T10)

Lesson context
This homework should follow class work which has involved shared writing of parts of a story and discussion of what makes a good ending.

Setting the homework
Tell the children that they will be reading a story about a school trip and writing their own ending of what happens. The activity is linked to the sheets on pages 105, 106 and 116. The four sheets could be used as a homework sequence.

Differentiation
Less able children could be provided with a series of blank frames on a rectangular shaped piece of paper to draw their own ending in the form of a cartoon strip. Encourage them to write a simple caption to accompany each picture.

Back at school
Ask different children to share their endings to the story and see how they compare.

p120 ALLITERATIVE SENTENCES

Objective
Write alliterative sentences. (Y2, T3, T11)

Lesson context
This activity provides children with an opportunity to write alliterative sentences. It should be used as a follow-up to a lesson in which the children have been reading nonsense rhymes and writing rhymes and sentences that play with the same sounds.

Setting the homework
Explain that the children will need to write sentences beginning with the same sound. They should use the characters in the pictures as a starting point. You might like to work through one example together, eg 'Winnie the wicked witch watches wiggly worms'.

Differentiation
This will largely be by outcome, with more able children producing longer and more adventurous sentences.

Back at school
Ask the children to share examples of their alliterative sentences with the rest of the class.

p121 FACT OR FICTION?

Objective
Distinguish fact from fiction. (Y2, T3, T13)

Lesson context
This homework should follow up a lesson or series of lessons looking at the differences between fact and fiction.

Setting the homework
Tell the children that they will be reading extracts from fiction and non-fiction. Explain that these are all about animals and that they will need to read them carefully to decide which are fact and which are fiction. They should cut each section out and place it onto a separate sheet of paper which they have divided into two columns, one for fiction and the other for non-fiction. Remind them to check that their extracts are in the appropriate place before they stick them down.

Back at school
Ask the children to show their completed work to the rest of the class. Discuss the choices that they have made for each category.

p122 FIVE WS: WHO, WHERE, WHEN, WHAT, WHY?

Objective
Write suitable questions. (Y2, T3, T14)

Lesson context
This activity should follow class work that has involved formulating questions, both orally and in writing, using the five questions beginning with w-.

Setting the homework
Explain to the children that they will be playing a game with their parents or helpers and that they will need to read the instructions together carefully before writing the questions. Ask the children to bring in examples of their questions to read to the class.

Differentiation
Less able children may need help with writing the questions. If this is the case, the game will require at least two other players: someone with whom they can play the game and someone to write the questions.

Back at school
Invite the children to read out their questions and ask the class to offer possible answers before the 'correct' answer is given.

p123 FIND THE TELEPHONE NUMBER

Objective
Locate information in an index. (Y2, T3, T15)

Lesson context
Use this homework to follow up a lesson which has required the use of alphabetical order skills to scan a page from an index, dictionary and so on to find a specific piece of information.

Setting the homework
Children will need access to a telephone directory (explain that they can find one in a public library if they do not have one at home). They will need to scan quickly for the correct alphabetical page and then look through for the specific name and initial. (The names included are very common and most of them should be found in most telephone directories, but you could adapt the sheet with names in your own local directory, if necessary.) Ensure the children understand that they should not phone any of the numbers they find.

Differentiation
For less able children, the number of names could be limited. Also, if the selection is restricted so that there is only one name for each initial letter, the task will be made easier (they will not need to use the second letter of the name in order to find the word alphabetically).

Back at school
If you have one or two old telephone directories at school, ask the children to demonstrate finding a name in a directory.

p124 FIND OUT WHERE

Objective
Use an index. (Y2, T3, T15)

Lesson context
This activity should be carried out after a lesson in which the children have used a non-fiction index to find information from a text.

Setting the homework
Explain to the children that they will need to answer the questions on the sheet by looking at the index that is provided. Tell them that the index has been taken from a non-fiction book about pets. Make sure the children understand that they will have to think clearly about some of the questions, for example which pet could be described as dangerous?

Differentiation
Less able children will need support in answering the questions, particularly the non-literal ones.

Back at school
Using an enlarged copy of the index 'All About Pets' on the homework sheet, ask different children to answer the questions.
(Answers: 1: pages 19, 20; 2: pages 23, 24; 3: pages 9, 10, 17, 18; 4: pages 19, 20; 5: pages 9, 10, 17, 18.)

p125 MAKE AN INDEX

Objective
Make an alphabetically ordered index. (Y2, T3, T15)

Lesson context
This activity is intended to follow on from a lesson in which the children have used a non-fiction index to find information from a text.

Setting the homework
Explain that the children will need to first put the words into alphabetical order, then write the toys and page numbers to make their own index.

Differentiation
Children who are less secure in their knowledge of the alphabet may find an alphabet strip on a card helpful in order to sort the items alphabetically.

Back at school
Invite the children to show their indexes to the rest of the class. Encourage them to discuss how easy they found the task.

p126 COVER STORY

Objective
Evaluate the usefulness of a book for its purpose: book covers. (Y2, T3, T18)

Lesson context
This activity should follow up class work that has involved children surveying a range of book covers, in each case to decide on the type of book and to predict the contents.

Setting the homework
Explain that the children will be looking closely at illustrations of book covers and then completing information in a grid. Tell them that sometimes they will write the title and sometimes the information contained in the book. They can include what is written on the blurb, as well as adding to this to include other information that may be contained, eg a book titled *Insects* could include information on types of insects as well as body parts and feeding habits.

Differentiation
Less able children could be asked to include information which is already stated.

Back at school
Invite the children to share the information about the books that they have inserted in the grid on the homework sheet. Encourage them to offer any extra ideas about the books' contents.

p127 NOTING THE FACTS

Objective
Make simple notes from a non-fiction text. (Y2, T3, T19)

Lesson context
This homework should follow a lesson in which you have modelled scanning for key information and writing the key points.

Setting the homework
Explain to the children that they will be reading an extract about maiasaurs (a type of dinosaur) and will need to write notes in the grid. You may like to provide an example (eg 'size when fully grown – 9 metres long').

Back at school
Ask selected children to share examples of notes they have made.

Matching sounds

- Underline the words which have the same sound as the bold part of the word on the left. The first one has been done for you.

town   Mum's new car was <u>brown</u> with grey seats.

g**oo**d   It was raining so I covered my head with the hood of my coat.

d**ar**k   It was so busy in Hull that we could not find anywhere to park the car.

t**oy**   Boys and girls played together happily.

n**ow**   The town was full of people.

c**ow**   David frowned as he looked at the page of sums.

c**ar**d   The sums were too hard for David.

oil   The snake coiled itself around the tree.

out   There were about twenty people on the bus.

Dear Helper,

Objective: to identify words that have the same vowel sounds and to recognise the common spelling patterns for oo, ar, oy and ow.

Look at the words on the left of the sentences together and say them aloud before trying to find words with the same vowel sound in the sentences. Draw your child's attention to the similar spelling patterns, eg 't<u>ow</u>n', 'br<u>ow</u>n'; 'g<u>oo</u>d,' 'h<u>oo</u>d'; 't<u>oy</u>', 'b<u>oy</u>s'.

Match it!

oil	b**oy**	t**oy**	c**oi**n
j**oy**	j**oi**n	destr**oy**	f**oi**l
g**oo**d	h**oo**d	w**oo**d	t**oo**k
n**ow**	c**ow**	br**ow**n	d**ow**n
r**ou**nd	**ou**t	ab**ou**t	sh**ou**t
p**ar**k	p**ar**t	c**ar**	j**ar**
f**ar**	t**ar**t	m**ar**ch	**ar**ch

How to play

- Cut out the word cards and turn them all face down.
- Take turns with another player to turn over two cards at a time.
- If your two cards have the same sound highlighted, keep them. (Remember that many sounds can be made using different letters in different words. For example, in **out** and **now** the letters **ou** and **ow** both make the same sound.)
- The player who has the most pairs when all the cards have been taken is the winner.

Dear Helper,

Objective: to understand the common spelling patterns for the sounds oo, ar, oy and ow.

Play the game with your child. Talk about the different ways in which the same sound can be spelled.

PHOTOCOPIABLE

Down town

- In the story below find the words with the sounds:

  ar (as in c**ar**)   **oo** (as in g**oo**d)   **oy** (as in b**oy**)   **ow** (as in c**ow**)

The car park was full. It took Mum ages to find a place.
We drove round and round looking for a space.

I hate going to town. It's always crowded, and by
the time you've found somewhere to park, there's no time
to look in the toy shop. Mum tries to keep me happy by
saying things like, "Be a good boy now, and we can have
something nice to eat as soon as we get back home."

I try to be good, but I spend most of the time
trudging around, counting the minutes until we can get
back to the car park and go home again.

- Make a list of each type of word in the grid below.

c**ar**	g**oo**d	b**oy**	n**ow**

Dear Helper,

Objective: to understand the common spelling patterns for the sounds oo, ar, oy and ow.
First, read the story aloud with your child. Then re-read it and make the lists together, helping your child to identify the words that go with each sound.

Odd one out

- Which word in each row is the odd one out, because it has a different sound highlighted? Put a ring round it.

g**oo**d	w**oo**d	**oi**l
owl	p**ar**t	n**ow**
cl**ow**n	**ou**t	c**oi**n
s**oo**t	f**oo**d	c**oo**k
b**ar**	c**ow**	**ar**t

t**oi**let	b**oy**	h**ow**	c**oi**n
b**oo**k	w**oo**l	p**oo**l	l**oo**k
d**ow**n	b**oo**t	t**ow**n	f**ou**nd
sp**oo**n	bl**oo**d	m**oo**n	r**oo**m
h**ar**d	d**ar**k	sc**are**	c**ar**d

- Make up some sets of words of your own with an odd one out in each set. Use the back of this sheet.

Dear Helper,

Objective: to investigate and classify words with the same sounds but different spellings.

Look at the words and say them aloud with your child. Identify which is the odd word out in each set. Repeat the words several times if your child experiences difficulty in hearing the sounds. Then help your child to think of 'odd one out' sets.

W
Name:

One to ten

- Read these rhymes with a helper and try to learn them.
  (You may know them already!)

One, two,   _____

Buckle my shoe.   _____

Three, four,   _____

Knock at the door.   _____

Five, six,   _____

Pick up sticks.   _____

Seven, eight,   _____

Lay them straight.   _____

Nine, ten,   _____

A big fat hen.   _____

_____   One, two, three, four, five,

_____   Once I caught a fish alive.

_____   Six, seven, eight, nine, ten,

_____   Then I let it go again.

_____   Why did you let it go?

_____   Because it bit my finger so.

_____   Which finger did it bite?

_____   This little finger on my right.

- Write down pairs of rhyming words from the poems
  in the space provided.

- Can you add some more rhyming words of your own?
  Use the back of this sheet.

PHOTOCOPIABLE

Dear Helper,

Objective: to investigate words with the same sounds but different spellings.

Read the poems and learn them together. Help your child to identify the rhyming words and to try to think of other words that would rhyme with them.

100 LITERACY HOMEWORK ACTIVITIES • YEAR 2 TERM 1

Number rhymes

- Read the numbers.

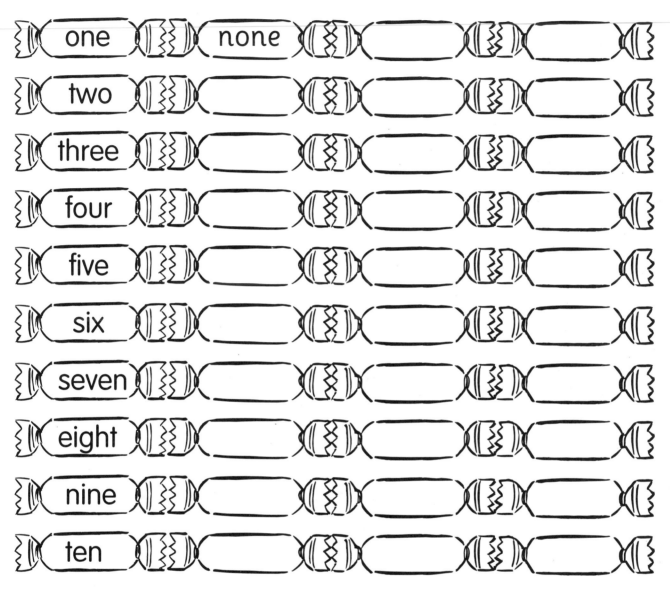

one   none

two

three

four

five

six

seven

eight

nine

ten

- Now see if you can write all these words next to
  the numbers which rhyme with them.
  One has been done for you.

tree	you	do	fun	drive	more
me	your	blue	mix	heaven	wait
tricks	then	eleven	fine	gate	fix
son	none	men	hive	late	

Dear Helper,

Objective: to investigate words with the same sounds but different spellings.

Read the numbers aloud together. Then read aloud each of the words in the list in turn. Ask your child which number the word rhymes with before they write it in the appropriate place.

PHOTOCOPIABLE

Words we use a lot

- Read the words below and then look at the piece of writing you've been given by your teacher.

- Underline the words in the piece of writing that can be found in the suitcase. For example:

  <u>Don't</u> <u>go</u> into the deep water, and stay <u>where</u> <u>we</u> <u>can</u> <u>see</u> <u>you</u>!

after	again	all	and	away
but	came	can	come	could
don't	for	from	go	had
just	like	me	my	not
now	once	over	people	see
so	them	they	time	to
too	very	was	were	where
who	with	would	yellow	you

Dear Helper,

Objective: to be able to read words that occur frequently.

Help your child to read the words above and the piece of writing that accompanies this homework. Ask your child to find the words in the text and underline them. Talk about the spellings of the words. If your child feels sufficiently confident, they could look at some words, one by one, cover them and then write them.

Spelling game

after	again	all	and	away
but	came	can	come	could
don't	for	from	go	had
just	like	me	my	not
now	once	over	people	see
so	them	they	time	to
too	very	eas	were	where
who	with	would	yellow	you

- Cut out the words to make 40 individual cards.

- Spread them out with the words face down.

- Take turns with another player to pick up a word and to say the word out loud. Don't show the word to the other player.

- If the other player can write the word down correctly, they keep the card. Check the spelling by looking at the card. If the word is not spelled correctly, put the card back, face down.

- The player who has the most cards when all of them have been picked up is the winner.

Dear Helper,

Objective: to be able to spell common words.

You may wish to play the game with a reduced number of cards. Make sure that there are plenty of words that your child can spell easily as well as a few which are more challenging. Add new words if your child is able to spell all of the words.

Solomon Grundy

- Read the poem.

Solomon Grundy,
Born on Monday,
Named on Tuesday,
Married on Wednesday,
Took ill on Thursday,
Worse on Friday,
Died on Saturday,
Buried on Sunday.
That was the end
Of Solomon Grundy.

- Now look carefully at the days of the week:

Monday   Tuesday   Wednesday   Thursday
Friday   Saturday   Sunday

- Write the correct day for each of the questions below:

When did Solomon Grundy die? _____

When did Solomon Grundy get married? _____

When was Solomon Grundy born? _____

When did Solomon Grundy take ill? _____

When did Solomon Grundy get worse? _____

When was Solomon Grundy named? _____

When was Solomon Grundy buried? _____

- Do you think Solomon Grundy only lived for a week?

Dear Helper,

Objective: to learn to spell the names of the days of the week.
Read the poem with your child and then do the activity together. Discuss the last question. Later, you may wish to help your child to learn the poem by heart.

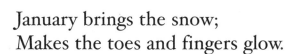

Months of the year

- Read the poem with a helper.
- Find the names of the months of the year.
  Say them in order.
- Then turn the sheet over and write the
  months of the year in order.

January brings the snow;
Makes the toes and fingers glow.

February brings the rain;
Thaws the frozen ponds again.

March brings breezes loud and shrill,
Stirs the dancing daffodil.

April brings the primrose sweet,
Scatters daisies at our feet.

May brings flocks of pretty lambs,
Skipping by their fleecy dams*.

June brings tulips, lilies, roses;
Fills the children's hands with posies.

Hot July brings cooling showers,
Strawberries and gilly-flowers.

August brings the sheaves of corn,
Then the harvest home is borne.

Warm September brings the fruit,
Sportsmen then begin to shoot.

Fresh October brings the pheasant;
Then to gather nuts is pleasant.

Dull November brings the blast,
Then the leaves are falling fast.

Chill December brings the sleet,
Blazing fire and Christmas treat.

Sara Coleridge

*Dams are mothers.

Dear Helper,

Objective: to learn the sequence and spellings of the months of the year.
Read the poem together and talk about what things the poet suggests each month brings. Ask your child to pick out the names of the months of the year. Then help them first to learn the names and then their spellings.

PHOTOCOPIABLE

Spell it!

said	you	come	was	could
half	have	laugh	love	many
once	one	people	should	some
their	two	want	water	who
would	your	blue	name	three

- Cut out the word cards and give them to your helper.
- Now see if you can find and spell each one.

Dear Helper,

Objective: to be able to spell common irregular words.

Spread the word cards out and ask your child to find words as quickly as possible. Say: 'How quickly can you find...?' Help your child to learn the spellings of the words using the LOOK, SAY, COVER, WRITE, CHECK method – your child should LOOK at the word carefully and SAY it, then turn the card over to COVER it and try to WRITE the word. Finally, they should CHECK to see if they have spelled it correctly. If not, ask them to try again (but not more than three times). If your child is able to spell all the words, they could try to arrange them in alphabetical order. You may need to talk about using the second and third letters when words have similar beginnings.

Alphabetical order

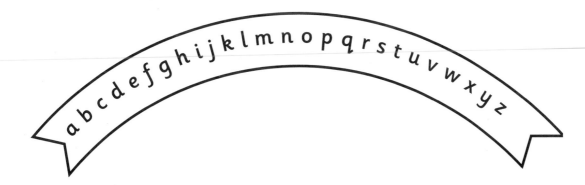

- Look at the words in each group, then arrange them in alphabetical order. The first one has been done for you.

two	once	people	<u>once people two</u>
who	laugh	have	_____
want	half	laugh	_____
love	some	should	_____
one	once	water	_____
would	want	many	_____
said	was	could	_____
you	come	who	_____
their	your	was	_____
have	who	two	_____

Dear Helper,

Objective: to be able to spell common irregular words and to develop understanding of alphabetical order. Read the groups of words together and help your child to arrange them in alphabetical order.

Label your home

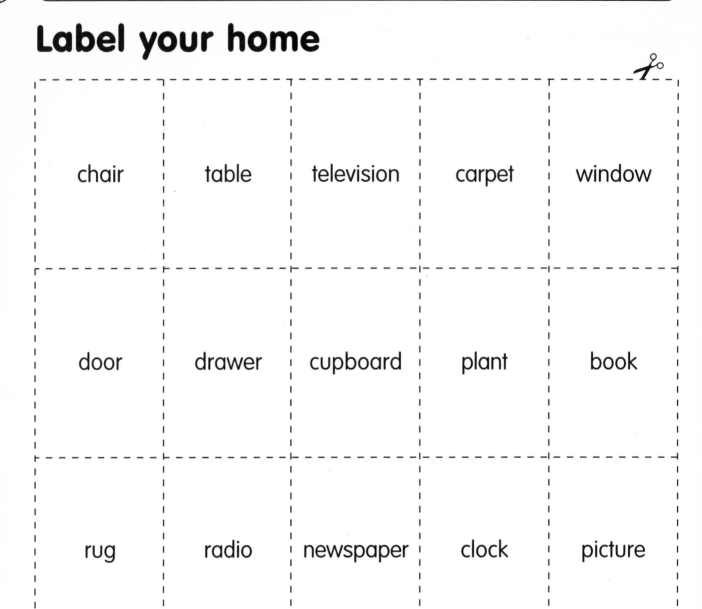

chair	table	television	carpet	window
door	drawer	cupboard	plant	book
rug	radio	newspaper	clock	picture

What to do

1 Cut out the labels. Use your scissors carefully.

2 Read the word on each label to your helper.

3 Place each label on or next to the correct object in your living room.

4 Did you use them all? If not, try to match the labels with the objects in other rooms at home.

Dear Helper,

Objective: to learn new words related to a particular topic: the home.

If your child has difficulty with some of the longer words, look together at the letters at the beginnings of the words and the sounds they represent. If you wish, you could add some labels of your own.

Find it!

chair	table	television	carpet	window
door	drawer	cupboard	plant	book
rug	radio	newspaper	clock	picture

What to do

1 Cut out the labels. Use your scissors carefully.

2 Spread the labels out on the floor.

3 Take turns with your helper to ask each other questions like:

● Can you find the word that begins with a **d** and means something you open and close to get in and out of a room?

● Which word ends with a vowel and means something that we listen to?

● We can watch our favourite programmes on it. What is it?

● It has pages and a cover. What is it?

● We keep things in it such as knives and forks. What is it?

● It can be found on the floor and its name rhymes with **hug**. What is it?

● You need to give it water if it is to grow. What is it?

Dear Helper,

Objective: to learn new words related to a particular topic: the home.

If you start the game, your child will soon catch on. You may need to read through all the words first. Try playing the game with other household items written out on labels.

At the seaside

deckchair	waves	sandcastle	seaweed
windbreak	umbrella	ice-cream	spade
bucket	beach		

What to do

1 Cut out the picture and word cards.

2 Spread the cards out – the picture cards face up and the word cards face down.

3 Turn over a word card. Read it and then match it to the correct picture card.

Choose the right word

- Read the sentences and choose the right words to fill in the spaces. The first one has been done for you.

(park/car/jar)

Mandeep opened a _____ jar _____ of jam when he made some tarts.

(boy/toy/house)

Chelsea sat next to a _____ called James.

(good/brown/hood)

When it rained, Ben put the _____ of his coat over his head.

(June/July/March)

_____ is the month which comes before April.

(cow/joy/join)

Becky jumped for _____ when she won the swimming race.

(park/car/brown)

Joshua and Jade played on the swings in the _____.

(joining/looking/shouting)

Ryan was looking forward to _____ the Cubs.

(part/far/wood)

Barnsley is not _____ from Sheffield.

(wood/now/out)

"Please take _____ your spelling books," said the teacher.

(took/good/march)

Hannah _____ her sister to the park.

Dear Helper,

Objective: to use awareness of grammar and context clues to predict missing words.

Read the sentences with your child and look at the words in brackets. Try saying the sentences using each word and then ask your child to choose the right one and write it in the space provided.

Cleaning your teeth

Now brush your teeth, taking care to clean all of them.

When the brush is wet, take the toothpaste and squeeze the tube until you have covered the tips of the bristles with paste.

Next, put your toothbrush under the tap.

Finally, put your toothbrush and toothpaste away and dry your face.

First take your toothbrush and turn on the cold tap.

Remember to brush up and down.

Rinse your mouth with water and turn off the tap.

Instructions often begin with words such as:

first   next   then   after   that   when   finally

They also often begin with verbs that tell us what to do.

- Read the instructions above, which are printed in the wrong order. Look especially at the first words in each sentence and then try to put the instructions into the right order. You don't need to write the instructions down, just cut each one out and then arrange the boxes in the right order.

Dear Helper,

Objective: to develop and reinforce knowledge of instructions and to look at words that link sentences.

Look at the instructions together and ask your child to read them with you and to you. Encourage them to experiment with arranging the order. When satisfied with the correct order, your child should stick the sentences down on a piece of paper.

Punctuate the passage

- Read the text and then put in full stops and commas. Some of the words that begin with capital letters may help you.

Edith Howcraft

My grandmother is called Edith Howcroft She was born on 28th December 1900 She was nearly three years old when the first aeroplane flew As a little girl she hardly ever saw cars but she sometimes rode on a train The trains were pulled by steam engines which made a lot of noise and filled the air with smoke steam and soot

She went to school in a village two miles from her home She had to walk across fields to get to school and she had to walk back again at lunchtime because there were no school dinners in those days Her mother used to walk across the fields and meet her and her sister and they used to have picnics in the summer

When she was twelve my grandmother had to leave school and get a job She worked for a shopkeeper delivering meat bread fruit and vegetables She remembers falling off her bike and cutting her knee and losing all of the food one cold wet winter day

At Christmas the only presents my grandmother had were oranges nuts apples and home-made rag dolls She says that even though her family had very little money they were very happy and she would not change a thing about her childhood

Dear Helper,

Objective: to read for sense and punctuation.

Read the text to your child and talk about it. Ask if anything is missing from the text. Talk about the way in which full stops tell us when sentences end and that one of the jobs of commas is to separate items in lists. Read the text with your child and ask them to tell you when full stops or commas might be included.

Name: [ ]

Jill and Jack

- Read the story.

It was a long way up the steep hill. The children, whose names were Jill and Jack, took turns to carry the bucket. In the distance, they could see the well.

"Can't we stop for a rest?" asked Jack after a few minutes.

"No," replied Jill. "We have to get the bucket of water to Mum quickly, if we want any dinner."

The children carried on climbing the hill. Below them they could see the town of Bilton, and they spotted their own house with smoke coming from the chimney.

Finally, they reached the top of the hill and lowered the bucket deep into the well. It took ages before they heard the bucket splash into the water. They pulled it up again and poured the water into their own bucket. As Jack tried to pick up the full bucket, he stumbled and fell. The water spilled as Jill tried to stop Jack from tumbling down the hill. She slipped and rolled down the hill after her brother.

"Ouch, that hurt!" grumbled Jack as he stood up at the bottom of the hill.

"Thank goodness we're both all right," said Jill. "Now we'd better climb all the way back to the top of the hill again!"

- Put a line under all the capital letters.
- Now sort the words out into two kinds:

Draw a ring ○ around those which have capitals because they begin sentences or speech.

Draw a box □ around those which have capitals because they are special names.

Dear Helper,

Objective: to revise knowledge about the use of capital letters.

Read the story with your child and identify the words that begin with capital letters. Talk about the reason for the capital letters. Do they signify a special name, the beginning of a sentence or paragraph, or the beginning of speech?

100 LITERACY HOMEWORK ACTIVITIES • YEAR 2 TERM 1

W

Find the capitals

- Look in your reading book and in other books, newspapers and magazines. Find words which begin with capital letters and write them down under one of the headings.

Beginning of a sentence	Name of a person	Name of a place	Name of day or month	Beginning of speech

Lost on the beach

- Read this story with your helper.

"Don't go into the deep water and stay where we can see you!"

I could hear my mother's words as I ran towards the sea across the crowded beach. I dashed past toddlers digging in the sand; skipped around parents and children who were building sandcastles; and walked carefully past sunbathers in case I kicked sand onto them.

The soft white sand, which was so pleasant to walk on, soon became stony as I neared the sea. The pebbles and rocks hurt my feet and I picked my way across the beach, all the time saying, "Ow, ow, ouch!"

After the stones, the sand was wet and covered with slippery seaweed. I tried to avoid walking on it, but once I almost slipped and fell over.

Finally, I reached the water's edge. The tide was coming in and children waited for the waves to come crashing towards them before running, screaming and laughing to try to avoid getting soaked. I joined in and managed to run away three times before an extra large wave came in too fast for me and washed over me as I stumbled. The water was cold and my teeth chattered, but I didn't mind. I was enjoying myself.

After about half an hour, I remembered my parents and decided I had better go back and tell them I was all right. They worried if they didn't know where I was. I turned my back on the sea and began to walk inland. The seaweed seemed to have almost disappeared but the stony part of the beach was as big as before and I felt my feet getting sore.

I stopped to rest and looked up the beach to where I thought my parents would be, but I could not see them at all. They had a blue and yellow windbreak and a matching umbrella to shade them from the sun. As I looked around, I could see dozens of umbrellas that were just like ours. I began to panic. I must have moved along the beach when I was playing, and now I did not recognise any of the people I could see. Everyone on the beach seemed so happy, but I was feeling very unhappy indeed.

Dear Helper,

Objective: to understand time and sequence in stories, ie what happened when.
Read the story together and talk about it. Discuss the order in which events take place. Then encourage your child to think about what might happen next.

What happened and when?

- Read the story frame below and think of a story that could go with it. Make notes in each section of your ideas.

One day I was

Suddenly, I heard a loud noise that

I looked around and saw

At first, I could hardly believe my eyes, but

Then

At last

- Now write the story in sentences. You can use the back of this sheet or a separate sheet of paper.

Dear Helper,

Objective: to understand time and sequential relationships in stories.

Help your child think of ideas for each section. Discuss the importance of trying out ideas and changing them if we think of better ones. Remind your child that writers rewrite and check spellings.

Reading instructions

- Read the instructions and look at the pictures.
  Then try to make the paper aeroplane.

Making a paper aeroplane

1. Fold a piece of paper in half. 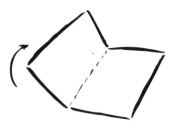	**5.** Fold each corner into the middle twice more. 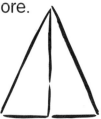
2. Open the paper out. 	**6.** Fold along the first crease so that the centre of the aeroplane sticks up. 
3. Take one corner of the paper and fold it to the centre of the paper to where the crease is. 	**7.** Fly your aeroplane by taking hold of the centre and throwing the plane upwards. 
4. Do the same with the corner next to it. 	

Dear Helper,

Objective: to read and follow instructions.

Look at the instructions together and ask your child to read them with you and to you. Make the paper aeroplane together.

How to play 'Concentration'

Monday	Monday	Tuesday	Tuesday
Wednesday	Wednesday	Thursday	Thursday
Friday	Friday	Saturday	Saturday
Sunday	Sunday	day	day
week	week	year	year

● Read the instructions and play the game.

1 Cut out the words.

2 Spread all the words face down on a table.

3 Players take turns to turn over two cards.

4 If a player turns over two cards which are the same, they keep those cards, which count as one 'trick'. If the cards are not the same, they should be turned back over.

5 When all of the cards have been taken, the player with the most tricks is the winner.

Tip
Try to remember where different cards are, so that when it comes to your turn it will be easier to make a pair!

PHOTOCOPIABLE

Dear Helper,

Objective: to read and follow simple instructions and to develop familiarity with days of the week.
Cut out the words. Look at the instructions together and then play the game.

Stick in the mud

- Read the instructions and then explain to someone how to play the game.

1 First decide who is going to be 'it'. You could do this by each putting a foot into a circle and asking one person to say a rhyme to decide. Here's one you could try:

> Mickey Mouse built a house underneath a tree
> Which number was it?
> One, two, three.

One person touches each foot each time they say a word. The person whose foot is touched on the word **three** is 'it'.

2 The person who is 'it' counts to ten while everyone else runs away.

3 After counting to ten, 'it' can chase the others.

4 When 'it' touches (tigs) someone's back, that person has to stand still with legs apart.

5 If a player who has not been 'tigged' crawls through the legs of someone who has, that person is released and can run away again.

6 'It' carries on until everyone has been 'tigged' and is standing still.

Dear Helper,

Objective: to read simple instructions for a game, and to learn and recite favourite poems.

Read the instructions with your child and then ask them to explain to you how to play the game. If possible, play the game with your child and others. You need at least three people to play. Talk about any rhymes you know which are used to decide who should go first.

Making a pancake

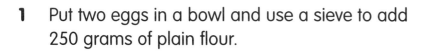

- Read the instructions for the recipe. Then use the table to show which ingredients and utensils are needed.

1 Put two eggs in a bowl and use a sieve to add 250 grams of plain flour.

2 Add half a litre of milk and beat with a whisk until smooth and creamy.

3 Heat a knob of butter in a frying pan until it melts.

4 Pour enough of the batter into the pan to cover the surface and use a spatula to turn the pancake when it starts to set.

5 When both sides are golden brown, take the pan away from the heat and use the spatula to lift the pancake onto a plate.

6 Sprinkle the pancake with sugar and use a lemon squeezer to dribble lemon juice over it.

7 Take a knife and fork and enjoy eating your pancake.

Ingredients	Utensils

Dear Helper,

Objective: to read simple written instructions and to learn new words related to a particular topic.

Talk with your child about ingredients and utensils. You could get out some items from your kitchen and ask your child physically to sort these into ingredients and utensils. Your child might indicate that scales and a measuring jug are needed to weigh the flour and measure the milk. If necessary, help your child to write the names of the ingredients and utensils in the boxes.

PHOTOCOPIABLE

Name:

Play the game

What you need
- a dice and a shaker
- different coloured counters for each player

How to play

1 Put a counter for each play at the 'start'.

2 Take turns to throw the dice.

3 Move the same number of spaces as the spots on the dice show.

4 If you land on a square which has instructions, follow them.

5 The winner is the first person to reach 'home'.

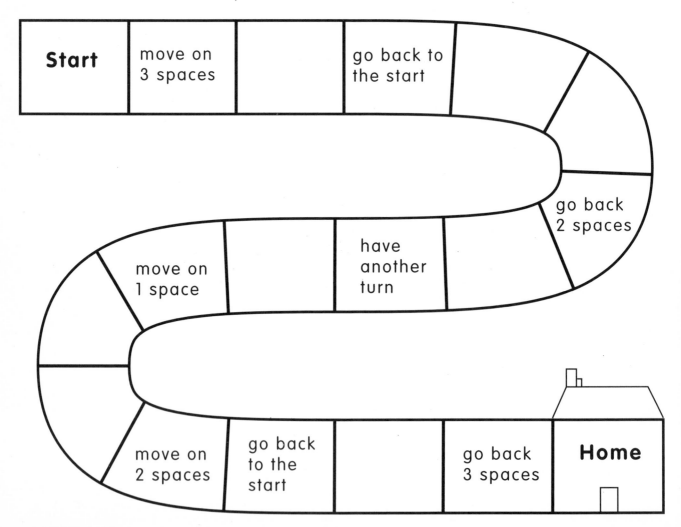

Dear Helper,

Objective: to read and follow instructions.

Play the game with your child. Look at the instructions together and ask your child to read them with you and to you.

Simon says!

Turn left	Turn right	Sit down	Jump
Stand still	Turn around and face the opposite way	Hop on your right foot	Turn all the way round
Touch your left knee with your right hand	Touch your right foot with your right hand	Touch your left ear with your right hand	Put your left hand in the air
Stand still	Touch your right ear with your left hand	Walk backwards 5 steps	Walk forwards 5 steps

What to do

1 Cut out the instruction cards. Use your scissors carefully.

2 Read the instructions on each card. If there are any you don't understand, talk about them with a helper.

3 Now turn the cards over and mix them up.

4 Choose six cards and hold them in your hand.

5 Read each one and perform the action.

Dear Helper,

Objective: to develop and reinforce knowledge of directions and instructions.

If necessary, offer your child help in reading and understanding the instructions, but do encourage them to try to work out what should be done. If you wish, you could add some instruction cards of your own.

PHOTOCOPIABLE

Name:

Writing instructions

- Make a paper aeroplane.

- Now write instructions for making the aeroplane in the left-hand boxes below. Begin your sentences with words such as:

  First   Next   Fold   Fly   Finally

- You might like to draw simple pictures in the right-hand boxes to illustrate each of the instructions.

- Ask someone to try making your paper aeroplane. If the person finds it easy to make the aeroplane, you have probably written good instructions!

Dear Helper,

Objective: to write clear instructions and test them out.

Ask your child to describe the process of making the aeroplane before writing it down. Ask questions such as 'What did you do first?' 'Which way did you fold the paper?' 'Does it matter if you do it this way or that way?'

Write your own recipe

● Look at the pictures and then write instructions
next to the numbers to go with each one.
Write a title for the recipe.

RECIPE FOR _____

1 _____

2 _____

3 _____

4 _____

5 _____

6 _____

7 _____

8 _____

Name:

Hide and seek

- Look at the pictures and write instructions to go
  with each one to explain how to play hide and seek.

Dear Helper,

Objective: to write simple instructions for a game.

Look at the pictures with your child and help them to write instructions that are simple and clear.

Write your own instructions

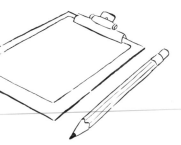

- Make a collection of instructions you can find around your home. For example, look for recipes and instructions for games.

- In the box below, write down some of the words that begin sentences in instructions.

- Now write some sentences which begin with the words you have found.

Dear Helper,

Objective: to write simple instructions.

Look at instructions with your child. Identify some of the words that begin instructions. Point out that these are often sequence words, such as 'first', 'then', 'after', or verbs that tell you what to do, such as 'mix', 'place', 'move', 'cut'.

Getting to school

- Tom wrote instructions for getting to school. Read them and see if Tom does the same things that you do.

1 First put on your coat.

2 Next, pick up your school-bag.

3 When you are ready to go out, say goodbye to anyone who is staying at home.

4 Now walk to school, taking care when crossing roads.

5 When you reach school, say hello to your friends.

6 Finally, when you hear the bell, go into school and hang your coat and school-bag in the cloakroom.

- Now write your own instructions for getting to school. Use some of these words to begin some of your sentences:

first **next** **now** **when** **finally**

1 _____

2 _____

3 _____

4 _____

5 _____

6 _____

Dear Helper,

Objective: to write simple instructions.

Read the instructions together and then help your child to write some which are appropriate to their journey to school. Talk about any words which are new to your child and help them to learn to spell them: by looking at the word, saying it, covering it up, writing it, then checking it.

Ooh, look at that!

- Look at the words in the list. They all contain **oo**.

  In some of the words the **oo** makes a sound like the **oo** in f**oo**d.

  In others the **oo** makes a sound like the **oo** in g**oo**d.

- Sort the words out and write them underneath **good** or **food** to show how they should be pronounced.

moon	fool	blood	soon	soot
shoot	room	stood	foot	cool
zoo	look	wool	roof	spoon
cook	tooth	mood	tool	hook
book	wood	broom	hood	crook

good

food

Dear Helper,

Objective: to revise reading and spelling of words which contain oo as in 'food' and oo as in 'good'.

Read the words with your child and talk about the two main different sounds which can be made using oo. Help your child to sort the words. If necessary, say the words aloud, exaggerating the oo sound.

Midnight adventure

Tip
Some have the letters **or** making the **or** sound, but in others the sound is made by other letters!

- Read this story about Ralph.
- Underline all the words that have an **or** sound in them.

The rain poured down as Ralph crept out of the door. He watched it fall and knew that he would soon be very wet. From somewhere in the dark woods an owl called. The more he thought about what he had to do, the more worried Ralph became. It was now or never.

There was a light in his brother Jack's room. He wished Jack would draw his curtains at night. Maybe he was watching him as he walked quickly across the lawn. Ralph hid in the shadows of the tall trees for three or four minutes, waiting to see if Jack had seen him. When he was sure that all was still and quiet, Ralph set off into the woods.

Suddenly, there was a crunching noise and a torch was shone into his face. Ralph shivered and pulled his warm coat tightly around himself as he heard someone say, "So you decided to come after all. Don't forget I warned you it would be dangerous!"

- Write down all the different letter combinations that make the **or** sound. Then write each of the words you underlined under the correct **or** sound letter group. For example, the **or** sound is made by the letters **ar** in **warm** and by **our** in **four**.

Dear Helper,

Objective: to identify the or sound in writing.

Read the short story to and with your child. Look for words which have an or sound tip them and help your child to make a list of them. Go on to sort the words according to the letters which are used to make the or sound. Talk about Ralph's adventure and discuss what might happen next.

100 LITERACY HOMEWORK ACTIVITIES • YEAR 2 TERM 2

Words for all

dirt	shirt	worth	hurt	worse
tall	all	more	wore	four
door	small	call	caught	thought
girl	burger	her	thirteen	purple
bought	fall	warn	dawn	walk
saw	jaw	floor	for	draw
stir	fir	word	first	driver
bird	baker	learn	heard	fur

- Read the words together. Some have an **or** sound in them and some have an **er** sound. What sound does **burger** have?

- Now cut out all the words and turn them face up. Take turns to pick up two words which have an **er** or **or** sound. Say the words aloud as you do so.

- When you know what all of the words say, turn them face down and take turns to turn over two at a time. If you turn two words over which have an **er** sound or two which have an **or** sound, keep them as a 'trick'. The player with the most tricks when all of the cards have been taken is the winner.

Take care! Some words (like **word**) have **or** in them but are pronounced with an **er** sound.

Dear Helper,

Objective: to identify the *or* and *er* sounds in writing as in 'door', 'more', 'four' and 'warm', and 'bird', 'heard', 'word' and 'her'.

Read the words together and talk about the parts of the words which make an *or* or *er* sound. Go on to play the matching games.

Charlotte, Charles and Chloe

The names below begin with **ch**, but **ch** has a different sound in each.

Charlotte   Charles   Chloe

- Read the sentences below and underline the words which have **ch** in them.

1   Whenever Grandad asks me what I would like from the sweet shop, I always choose chocolate.

2   The chef wore a tall, white hat and an apron when he chopped the onions and sliced the cheese.

3   Father Christmas is a jolly character with a beard covering his chin.

4   The choir sang the Christmas carol Chloe chose.

5   Charlie's chum Chris was a cheerful chap.

- Write the words which you underlined underneath the word below which has the same **ch** sound.

Charles	Charlotte	Chloe

Dear Helper,

Objective: to read and spell words beginning with the letters *ch*.

Read the sentences with your child. Help your child to distinguish between the different sounds which *ch* can represent and assist them in writing the *ch* words under the appropriate name.

Chef's chocolate

- Look at the words in the list. Read them carefully and then decide which **ch** sound they each have and write them next to the correct picture. One has been done for you.

chat	chip	choice	parachute
chrome	chase	child	chair
Christopher	chin	choir	chart
each	ache	machine	Michelle
chef	cherry	Christmas	anchor

chat

chocolate

chef

chemist

- Add some more **ch** words to the pictures. You could use a dictionary to help you to find more words.

Dear Helper,

Objective: to read and spell words containing the letters *ch*.

Look at the words which include *ch* and say them with your child. Next look at the words 'chocolate', 'chef' and 'chemist' under the pictures. Talk about the different sounds which *ch* can make. Now help your child to list each of the *ch* words next to the picture that has the same *ch* sound. If your child finishes the task easily, try adding some more words. You could look in a dictionary together or in your child's reading book. Talk about which sound for *ch* seems to be the most common.

What a collection!

- All of these words contain **ph** or **wh**. Say them aloud.

- Write the **ph** words in the elephant and the **wh** words
  in the whale.

pheasant	elephant	whale	photograph	telephone
who	what	when	where	why
which	graph	phantom	Philip	Stephanie

- Collect some other **ph** and **wh** words. Look for them in
  your reading book and in other texts. Learn how to say
  the words and try to find out what they mean. Write
  them in either the whale or the elephant.

- Choose two **wh** words and two **ph** words and use them
  each in a sentence. Write your sentences on the back
  of this sheet.

Dear Helper,

Objective: to read and spell words containing the letters *wh* and *ph*.

Read the words aloud with your child and talk about the ways in which we usually pronounce the sounds *wh*
and *ph*. Help your child to look at newspapers, books and so on to find more words which include *wh* or *ph*.
Help your child to say the words correctly.

Time to rhyme

- Look at the words around the table.
- Now look at the words in the table.
- Write each of the words from around the table next to the word in the table with which it rhymes.

den   do

then   there   sly

laugh   ten

wh or ph word	rhyming words
when	
why	
where	
who	
phone	
graph	
pheasant	
phase	

groan   hair

try   days

dry   my

high   pleasant   alone   two

men   moan   fair

Word sums

- Look at the words below. They are all made by joining two words together.

- Write the two words that make up each word in the space next to the words. The first one has been done for you.

football = foot + ball

playground =

lawnmower =

dustbin =

postbox =

suitcase =

breadboard =

treetop =

hairbrush =

handbag =

toothbrush =

armchair =

Dear Helper,

Objective: to split familiar compound words into their component parts.

Compound words are words which are made up of two words joined together, for example 'hair' + 'brush' = 'hairbrush'; 'foot' + 'ball' = 'football'; 'play' + 'ground' = 'playground'. Look at the compound words together and read them aloud together. Ask your child to try to find the two words which go together to make each compound word.

Making compound words

every	bed	track	grand	cloth
father	one	room	table	suit
book	where	any	mother	case
motor	news	bath	bike	paper
tooth	hair	brush	no	paste

● How many compound words can you make using the words above? You may use each word as many times as you like. Write your compound words below.

Dear Helper,

Objective: to be able to build compound words using component parts.
Read all of the words together. You might like to cut them out. Try different pairs of words next to each other and see if they make compound words. If in doubt, use a dictionary to check if the words you have made exist.

Find the compound words

- Read the text and underline the compound words.
- Write them down in the table and write the two words which make up each one.

Everyone was enjoying the sunshine. Everywhere you looked you could see sunbathers. Some were reading newspapers, some were sitting on deckchairs sleeping, and some were building sandcastles.

Children played football or cricket. It was as if the seaside was a giant playground. Instead of schoolteachers on playground duty, there were lifeguards to make sure everybody was safe.

compound word	words which make the compound word
	+
	+
	+
	+
	+
	+
	+
	+
	+
	+
	+
	+
	+

Dear Helper,

Objective: to be able to split familiar compound words into their component parts.

Read the text together and try to identify the compound words. Help your child to write the compound words and their constituent parts.

How many syllables?

- Look at the table below. Read the words in each column.

one syllable	two syllables	three syllables	four syllables
dog	rabbit	elephant	rhinoceros
Beth	Gopal	Oliver	Alexandra
York	London	Nottingham	Middlesborough

- Now see if you can fill in all of the spaces with words that have the right number of syllables. You will probably find it easier to find words with one or two syllables than to think of words with three or four.

! Tip
You could look in an atlas or a newspaper for ideas.

Dear Helper,

Objective: to identify and count syllables in multisyllabic words and to note syllable boundaries in speech and writing.

Remind your child about syllables by clapping the syllables in names and familiar objects. For example, 'Liv-er-pool' has three syllables and would need three claps, while 'Can-ter-bu-ry' has four and would need four claps. By developing an appreciation of syllable boundaries, your child should find it easier to break up difficult words when reading or spelling.

Matching syllables

Monday	Tuesday	Wednesday	Thursday
Friday	Saturday	Sunday	January
February	March	April	May
June	July	August	September
October	November	December	one
two	three	four	five
six	seven	eight	nine
ten	eleven	twelve	thirteen
fourteen	fifteen	sixteen	seventeen
eighteen	nineteen	twenty	yellow
purple	blue	green	orange
Manchester	Liverpool	Newcastle	Bath

- Cut out the words and spread them out so that you can see them all.

- Put them into four groups:

  one-syllable words   two-syllable words

  three-syllable words   four-syllable words

Dear Helper,

Objective: to identify and count syllables in words.

Remind your child about syllables by clapping the syllables in names and familiar objects. For example, 'Sept-em-ber' has three syllables and would need three claps, while 'Febr-u-ar-y' has four and would need four claps. If your child finds the game easy, you could add some more words. You may wish to add some more four-syllable words.

The secret garden in the city

- Read about the secret garden. Then look at the words that are written at the top and bottom.

- Find the words and draw lines from them to the places where you can see them in the piece of writing about the secret garden. One has been done for you.

it   but   in   as   where   day

Somewhere in the noisy, busy city where people hurry from place to place is a little garden. The garden is quiet and peaceful and at one end is a fountain and a pond. In the pond are goldfish. There are large orange ones and tiny black and orange ones.

Very few people know about the garden, even though it is near to the huge church which thousands of people visit every day.

All you can hear in the garden is the tinkling of the water from the fountain as it falls into the pond, and the rustling of the wind in the trees and the birds singing. I love the city and the shops and houses, but the secret garden is my favourite place.

people   little   is   are   ones   very   water   about

Dear Helper,

Objective: to be able to read words that occur frequently.
Read the text together and talk about any words that your child finds difficult. Read the words that are listed and then help your child to find matching words in the text.

Opposites

- Look at the two lists of words. Draw lines to join the words that have opposite meanings. One has been done for you.

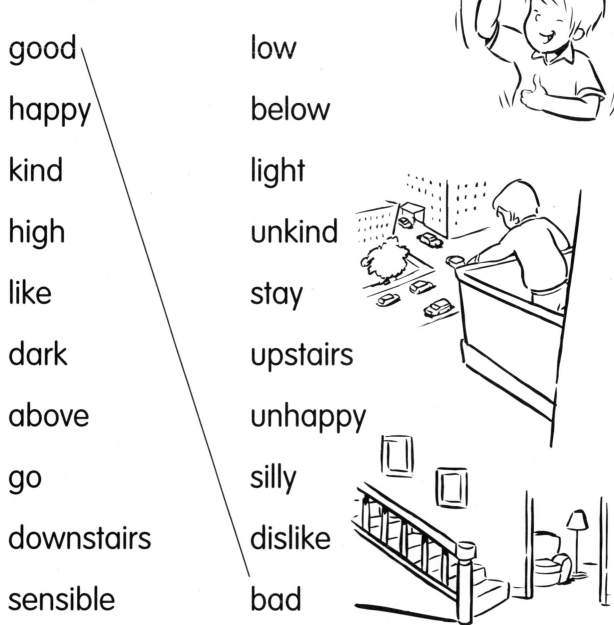

good	low
happy	below
kind	light
high	unkind
like	stay
dark	upstairs
above	unhappy
go	silly
downstairs	dislike
sensible	bad

- Now make your own jumbled lists of opposites and join the pairs with lines.

Dear Helper,

Objective: to understand the use of opposites and to discuss differences of meaning.

Look at the words in each list together and then work out the opposites for each one. At school, your child will have heard the term antonyms for opposites, so you can use this term with them. Talk about opposites and try saying some simple words (that have opposites) and asking your child to tell you some possible opposites.

Find the opposite

- Look at the list of words and write **at least one** word for each that has an opposite meaning. The first one has been started for you.

little	big, large
hard	
empty	
in	
up	
some	
hot	
raw	
obey	
near	
undo	
agree	
before	
with	
appear	
first	

Dear Helper,

Objective: to understand the use of opposites and to discuss differences of meaning.

Look at the words in the left-hand column with your child and read them aloud. Ask your child to suggest opposites for each one. At school, your child will have heard the term antonyms for opposites, so you can use this term with them. There may be more than one opposite for some words (eg the opposite of 'hard' could be 'soft' or 'easy'). Help your child to write the opposites in the boxes next to the words and discuss spellings.

Stop throwing paint!

- Choose one of the words in the box to complete each of the sentences. There may be more than one word that fits, but you should choose the one which you think fits best to write in the space.

answered   shouted   asked   replied   whispered   grumbled   yelled

"Stop throwing paint at each other!" _____ the

teacher.

"Have you got any red paint left?" _____ Lisa.

"No," _____ Ryan.

"There's never any red when I need it," _____

Lisa.

"Why don't you pinch some from David's table while he's not

looking?" _____ Ryan.

"Because Miss Cole will be cross if she finds out,"

_____ Lisa.

Suddenly a voice boomed from behind the children. "Yes, Lisa,

you're quite right. Miss Cole will be very cross if she catches you taking

other people's paint!" _____ Miss Cole in the angry

voice which she hardly ever used.

Dear Helper,

Objective: to choose words that are appropriate to the text to fill the spaces.
Read the dialogue with your child and look at the spaces. Help your child to identify the words that could be used to fill in the spaces. Encourage your child to think about what each person said and to take this into account when choosing the appropriate verb.

Painting

- Read about painting. Then fill in the spaces using the words below.

I love painting more than anything else we do at school. I really like having a

big white piece of _____ and being able to choose where to

start my picture. _____ I like to mix colours to make

_____, more interesting colours. My favourite

_____ is _____ and I can make hundreds of

different greens by mixing _____ and blue in different ways.

Once I painted a forest and I used all sorts of different greens to

_____ the trees look real.

　　　Our paint trays only have red, yellow, blue, black and white in them. We

have to mix the different powder paints together to make new colours. When

we _____ to paint, we always paint a background first. I

_____ to paint a light blue background and

_____ start to add details to my pictures. One

_____ I _____ like to be a famous painter and

sell my pictures for thousands of pounds to _____ who would

hang them on their walls and feel happy every _____ they

looked at _____.

green	new	colour	yellow	make
like	start	paper	then	would
people	day	time	them	first

Dear Helper,

Objective: to choose words that are appropriate to the text to fill the spaces.

Read the text together and talk about any words that your child finds difficult. Look at the words in the box underneath the text and read them. Re-read the text and help your child to choose appropriate words to fill in each space. In many cases there may be more than one word that might fit.

PHOTOCOPIABLE

Name:

Who said that?

- Look at the pictures and then look at the words that the people said. Complete the sentences by writing the verb in the past tense and the name of the person in the spaces provided. (The past tense of **say** is **said** and the past tense of **shout** is **shouted**.)

Miss Hardcastle

Thomas

Sarah Shaw

Mrs Morgan

Mr Davies

Ranjit

"Now just wait there until I tell you it's safe to cross,"

_____. (say)

"Oh thank you. It's just what I wanted,"

_____. (cry)

"This is delicious. I've never tasted anything like it,"

_____. (mumble)

"Now look, you are supposed to fetch the stick when I throw it!"

_____. (grumble)

"It's mine I tell you. You can't wear it!"

_____. (shout)

Please can I have one? I promise I won't want anything else,"

_____. (plead)

Dear Helper,

Objective: to use verb tenses with increasing accuracy in writing.

Look at the pictures with your child and then read the speeches together. Help your child to complete the sentences by adding the correct verb form and the name of the person whom they think made each speech.

What's black and white and read all over?

"What is black and white and read all over?" asked Shamin.

Jenny thought for a moment and then replied, "I don't know. What is black and white and red all over?"

"A newspaper!" said Shamin with a smile.

Jenny looked puzzled. "But newspapers aren't red," she grumbled.

Shamin laughed. "They're not red the colour, but they are read because people read them."

Jenny groaned. She decided she would get her own back after Shamin's joke. "Right Shamin, if you're so clever let's see if you can do this: Wednesday is a very hard word. Can you spell it?"

"Easy," laughed Shamin, "w-e-d-n..."

Before she could say any more, Jenny interrupted. "No, you've got it wrong!"

"Of course I haven't. It's w-e-d..."

Jenny interrupted again. "No it isn't. Fancy you not even being able to spell a simple word like it."

"But you asked me to spell Wednesday," complained Shamin.

"No I didn't. What I said was, 'Wednesday is a very hard word. Can you spell it?' It is spelled i-t."

Now it was Shamin's turn to groan.

- Underline all of the words that the girls spoke.
- Now take the part of one of the girls and ask your helper to be the other one. Have the conversation that Jenny and Shamin had, but remember only to say the words that they actually spoke.

Dear Helper,

Objective: to identify speech marks in reading and understand their purpose.
Read the dialogue with your child and look at the speech marks. Help your child to identify the words that are spoken, then hold the conversation together.

PHOTOCOPIABLE

Make a speech!

- Look at the pictures and write a conversation between the characters. Use speech marks to show which words were spoken. The first box has been done for you.

	"Oh no," cried Luke, "I can't find my money!"

Objective: to understand the purpose of speech marks and to use them in shared writing.

Look at the pictures with your child and talk about what is happening. Encourage your child to think about what each person might be saying and help them to write dialogue. Use speech marks to show which words are actually spoken.

Changing sentences

- Read the sentences and then write them again so that they have an opposite meaning.

Kate ran as quickly as she could.

Levi loved going to the dentist.

Mustafa liked playing football and hockey.

Jamie was the best cricketer in the class.

Lauren agreed with Grace that they should go swimming.

Holly closed the door.

Ewan and Oscar took the train from Taunton to Truro.

Dear Helper,

Objective: to understand the use of opposites and to discuss differences of meaning.

Read the sentences together and talk about the words that could be changed to change the meaning of the sentences. In some sentences more than one word might be changed. At school, your child will have heard the term antonyms for opposites, so you can use this term with them.

Name:

Descriptions

- From the words below, choose a subject and at least two adjectives and then write a sentence which describes the subject. See if you can write sentences for every subject. Here is an example:

I have a happy, pretty friend.

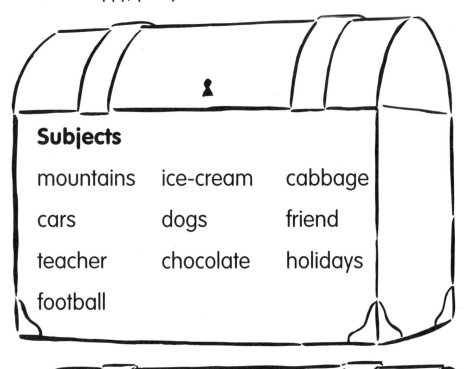

Subjects

mountains	ice-cream	cabbage
cars	dogs	friend
teacher	chocolate	holidays
football		

Adjectives

big	lovely	tasty	fun
small	short	delicious	friendly
happy	tall	clever	pretty
sad	heavy	horrible	kind
expensive	dirt		

Dear Helper,

Objective: to write simple descriptions and to encourage the use of simple sentences in own writing.

Read each set of words with your child and then help them to write sentences in which adjectives are used to describe the subjects. You may wish to add further subjects or adjectives.

Adjectives for Andrew

- Read the description together.

> Andrew looked sad as he carried his dirty, torn coat over his shoulder. The heavy rain had left muddy puddles on the path and his black shoes were filthy. He and his friend James should never have tried to jump over the wide stream. The water had been cold and Andrew had been soaked right up to his waist. His white shorts were now brown and mud-covered. Andrew knew that his parents would be furious when they saw him.

- Now answer the questions.

Which adjective tells you that Andrew was unhappy? _____

Which adjective tells you that Andrew's coat was damaged? _____

Which adjective tells you what the puddles were like? _____

Which adjectives describe Andrew's shoes? _____

Which adjective describes the stream? _____

Which adjectives describe Andrew's shorts before and
after he fell into the stream? _____

Which adjective describes how Andrew's parents will
feel when they see him? _____

- On the back of this sheet, write two sentences that describe what happens when Andrew's parents see him. Remember to use adjectives to improve your description.

Dear Helper,

Objective: to write simple descriptions and to encourage the use of simple sentences in own writing.
Read the text with your child and then help them to read the questions and identify the adjectives. Finally, help your child to write sentences to describe Andrew's encounter with his parents.

PHOTOCOPIABLE

Two different people?

- Read about Jordan. Then change the words that are in bold so that, instead of being unpleasant, Jordan is a pleasant person. Write about the pleasant Jordan in the box.

Mean Jordan

Jordan was a very **mean** boy. He **never** gave his friends **any** sweets and he **never** shared his crisps. He had **few** friends and **no one** liked him very much. The only time he was **happy** was when another child fell over or got into trouble with a teacher.

Pleasant Jordan

- Write down in pairs the bold words from 'Mean Jordan' and the opposite words (antonyms) which you used in 'Pleasant Jordan'. Use a separate sheet of paper.

Dear Helper,

Objective: to understand the use of opposites and to discuss differences of meaning.

Read the text together and talk about the words in bold that will alter its meaning if they are changed. Go on to write pairs of opposites that include the ones from the original text and the ones used to change its meaning. At school, your child will have heard the term antonyms for opposites, so you can use this term with them.

Missing mouse

- Read the story together and then talk about how you think it might end. Write down your ending on a separate sheet of paper.

"Why can't they leave the poor thing alone?" muttered Amy to herself.

She held the tiny mouse in her hands, taking care to keep it hidden under her coat. She was sure that it was trembling. It must have been frightened of her, but Amy would never hurt it.

All around her people were yelling and shouting and calling things like: "Over there! I think I saw it." The mouse had appeared in the classroom just as the children were getting ready to go out to play. Everyone had rushed in from the cloakroom when they heard Mrs Brady screaming. They had found their teacher standing on a chair looking around herself nervously.

The caretaker had been fetched and so had Miss Fleming and Miss Urmston. The adults and most of the children rushed around the room looking for the mouse. Only Amy knew where it was. She had seen it under her desk and had picked it up quickly before anyone had a chance to see. Now she wanted to protect it from all the people who wanted to catch it.

Dear Helper,

Objective: to predict story endings.
Read the story together and talk about any words that your child finds difficult. Discuss possible endings for the story before your child begins writing.

PHOTOCOPIABLE

Name:

Character sketches

Daisy is a happy, smiling, fair-haired girl. She likes to wear jeans and a T-shirt and loves to play football.

Rashid has dark hair that is always smartly combed. He dresses smartly and enjoys playing tennis.

Adam rarely combs his hair and he seems to love getting as dirty as possible whenever he goes out to play. His clothes are always full of holes.

Mrs Owen wears a thick coat whenever she goes out, even when it is hot and sunny. She always seems to be in a hurry and usually looks rather serious.

Natalie is always being cross with people. She has long, dark hair which she wears in a pony tail.

Mr Ferguson is always looking at his watch and looking worried. He has a moustache and wears smart suits and ties.

- Cut out the descriptions and the pictures. Read the descriptions of the characters and match them to the pictures. When you have done this, try writing a character sketch of someone you know and drawing a picture to go with it.

Dear Helper,

Objective: to identify and describe characters.

Read each of the descriptions with your child and then help them to decide which of the pictures fits each description. Look, in particular, at the adjectives and see if they are reflected in the pictures. Help your child to write a character sketch for someone else and to draw a matching picture.

Hands

- Read this poem about hands.

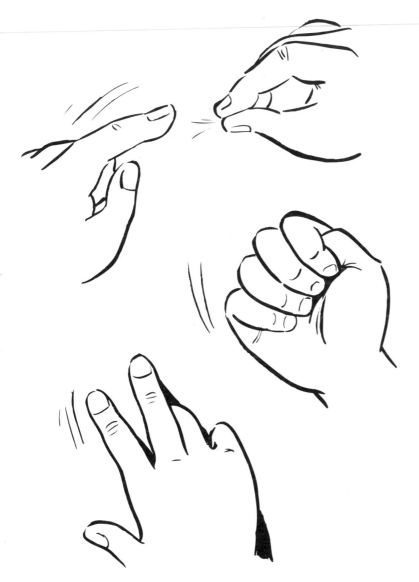

Hands
handling
dangling in water
making and shaking
slapping and clapping
warming and warning
hitting and fitting
grabbing and rubbing
peeling and feeling
taking and breaking
helping and giving
lifting
sifting sand
hand holding
hand.

Peter Young

- Lots of the verbs in the poem end with **-ing**. Think of some other verbs ending with **-ing** that show what hands can do. Write them on the back of this sheet.

- Try writing your own poem using lots of **-ing** verbs to describe things which hands can do.

Dear Helper,

Objective: to read poems aloud and discuss them.

Read the poem together and talk about it. Look at the verbs that end with *-ing* and talk about what they mean. Try writing a short poem together about what hands can do. Don't worry about making it rhyme. Concentrate on finding appropriate words (eg 'pinching', 'pointing', 'knocking', 'touching') and using them.

Winter morning

Winter is the king of showmen,
Turning tree stumps into snowmen
And houses into birthday cakes
And spreading sugar over lakes.
Smooth and clean and frosty white,
The world looks good enough to bite.
That's the season to be young,
Catching snowflakes on your tongue.
Snow is snowy when it's snowing,
I'm sorry it's slushy when it's going.

Ogden Nash

● Read the poem together and then answer the questions.

1 What is the name of the poet who wrote 'Winter morning'?

_____

2 Which word rhymes with **white** in the poem?

_____

3 Which word rhymes with **snowing** in the poem?

_____

4 Which word rhymes with **young** in the poem?

_____

5 How does the poet describe snow when it is going?

_____

6 Which line of the poem do you like best?

_____

Dear Helper,

Objective: to discuss poems using appropriate terms.
Read the poem together and then talk about it. Look at it again and then help your child to answer the questions. You and your child may wish to write some sentences or lines of verse to describe winter.

Books are great!

- Read the poem aloud and discuss what it's about.
- Identify the rhyming words and write them down.

CHORUS:
Books are great! Books are fun!
Books let you do what you've never done!
Books are cool! Books are in!
Books let you go where you've never been!

Read a good mystery, solve a good crime!
Read about history, go back in time!
Read about outer space, land on Mars!
Read about an auto race, zoom with the cars!

CHORUS

Read about a haunted house, shake to your knees!
Read about a cat and mouse, run for the cheese!
Read about a lost dog, where can it be?
Read about a giant frog under the sea!

CHORUS

Read a very funny book, blues go away!
Read a bright, sunny book on a rainy day!
Read a goodnight book, just before bed,
Let a sleep-tight book dance in your head!

CHORUS

Meish Goldish

Dear Helper,

Objective: to identify and discuss patterns of rhyme.

Read the poem together and talk about it. Look together for the pairs of rhyming words and write them down on a separate sheet of paper. In the poem, 'in' and 'been' rhyme. Talk about this and discuss the way in which 'been' would be pronounced to create the rhyme. Talk about the way in which the same sounds can be made using different letters, eg 'done' and 'fun'.

Noses

- Read the poem together.
- Find the sets of rhyming words. Write them down and discuss their different spellings.

I looked in the mirror
and looked at my nose:
it's the funniest thing,
the way it grows
stuck right out where all of it shows
with two little holes where the breathing goes.

I looked in the mirror
and saw in there
the end of my chin
and the start of my hair
and between there isn't much space to spare
with my nose, like a handle, sticking there.

If ever you want
to giggle and shout
and can't think of what
to do it about,
just look in the mirror and then, no doubt,
you'll see how funny YOUR nose sticks out!

Aileen Fisher

Dear Helper,

Objective: to identify and discuss patterns of rhyme in a poem.

Read the poem with your child. Talk about the groups of rhyming words and write them down on a separate sheet of paper. Look at the different ways in which the rhyming parts of the words may be spelled.

Write a poem

- Look at the poem below. It has been started but many words are missing. Use your own words to complete the poem. There are three verses.

When I grow up I want to be
A teacher like the one who teaches me.
I'll give the children sums to do

_____ too.

_____ chalk

_____ walk.

_____ day,

_____ play.

_____ hours

_____ flowers.

And when I get home at night,

_____ .

Dear Helper,

Objective: to use structures from poems as a basis for writing.
Read the beginning of the poem together and talk about it. Look together for the pairs of rhyming words. Work together to complete the poem, using as many of your child's ideas as possible.

Shopping at the supermarket

- In this flow chart the boxes are in the wrong order. Cut them out and stick them onto a piece of paper in the right order. Draw arrows between the boxes to make a flow chart like this one.

Go to the checkout.

↓

Pay for the things you have bought.

↓

Find a trolley.

↓

Put things in bags after the assistant has scanned them. Put the bags in your trolley.

↓

Choose the food you want to buy.

↓

Go into the supermarket.

Dear Helper,

Objective: to produce a simple flow chart which explains a process.

Read the information in each box with your child and then cut out the boxes. Discuss the logical order for the boxes and then help your child to stick the boxes onto a sheet of paper to produce a flow chart similar to the one above.

Make your own flow chart

- Choose a process for making something.
- Fill in the boxes in the flow chart to show the order in which things should be done. Here is an example to help you.

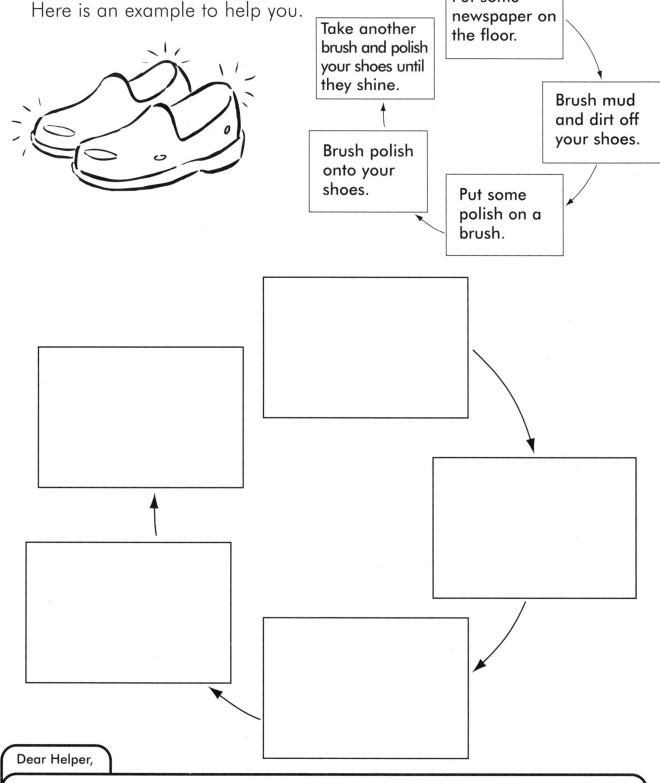

Put some newspaper on the floor.

Brush mud and dirt off your shoes.

Take another brush and polish your shoes until they shine.

Brush polish onto your shoes.

Put some polish on a brush.

Dear Helper,

Objective: to produce a simple flow chart which explains a process.

Look at the sample flow chart together, then decide upon another process that could be explained using a flow chart. Discuss the logical order for the boxes and then ask your child to fill in the flow chart.

Fred's bread and Doctor Deer

- Read the two poems with your helper.
- Find all the words that have the letters **ea** in them.
  Say the words and listen carefully to the different sounds.
  List them at the bottom of the page – choose the correct
  column each time. Two have been done for you.

Fred's bread

Ed said to Ned,
And Ned said to Ted,
And Ted said to Fred,
"This bread is red!"
Fred said to Ted,
"It's not just red,
It's heavy as lead."
"Must be the weather,"
Said Heather,
And she made the bread
Instead.
"Light as a feather!"
Said Heather.
Ed, Ned and Ted
Buried the red bread.
Fred went to bed
Instead.

Doctor Deer's ear and hearing clinic

"Dear Doctor Deer,"
Said Mr Steer,
"I fear I've lost
My hearing."
"You'll hear
Quite clear,"
Said Doctor Deer,
"If you
take off
your ear-ring!"

Sarah Hayes

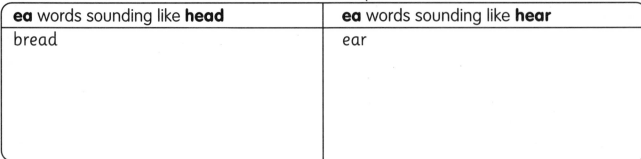

ea words sounding like **head**	**ea** words sounding like **hear**
bread	ear

Dear Helper,

Objective: to be able to identify different sounds made by the same letters.

Read the two poems carefully with your child and help them to find all the words containing the letters ea. Say the words aloud with them and talk about the different sounds made by the letters ea. Now help your child to list separately all the words that sound the same.

100 LITERACY HOMEWORK ACTIVITIES • YEAR 2 TERM 3

Ea snap

! Tip
Say the words aloud slowly.

W

head	ear	dead	hear
thread	eat	bread	seat
lead	dear	spread	clear
beach	deaf	reach	steady
team	fear	meal	idea

- Cut out the cards above.
- Play 'Snap' by matching the words that have the same **ea** sound.

Dear Helper,

Objective: to be able to match ea words by their sound.

Cut out the cards and shuffle them. Give half the cards to your child and take it in turns to turn a card over. Shout 'Snap' if both words have the same ea sound (either ea as in 'head' or ea as in 'ear'). If the person who shouts first is correct, they keep the two cards. The player with the most cards at the end is the winner.

Name:

Choose a word, make a sentence

- Choose four words from the list. Write four sentences using each of the words you have chosen. Here is an example using about:

He was excited about the trip.

about	again	another
because	been	could
first	going	have
make	next	people
said	saw	school
they	was	with

1 _____

2 _____

3 _____

4 _____

Dear Helper,

Objective: to be able to spell words that occur frequently.

First, ask your child to read the list of words to you. Then ask your child to choose four of the words and write a sentence for each of them. By writing them in the context of a sentence, your child will show their understanding of the meaning of the words. Encourage your child to check their spelling by looking back at the list. If your child is able, ask them to write more than four sentences, continuing on the back of the sheet.

Sounds of the city

- Read the poem below.
- Underline the words in each verse that rhyme.
- Some of the words that rhyme have different spellings for the same sound. Which words are these?

Scamper, scuttle,
Stop and stare,
Cities echoing sounds in the air.

Spring and stretch,
Stride and fuss,
Busy people rushing for a bus.

Circus in the city,
Dresses for the clown,
Stampeding horses make people frown.

Ice-cold drinks,
Sun beats down,
Sweltering people rush out of town.

Wendy Jolliffe

- Now write a list of all the words that have
  the sound **s** in them:

The fox and the crow

- Read the story of the fox and the crow.

Once an old crow stole a piece of cheese. She carried it to the nearest tree and perched on a high branch. She was just about to eat it when she heard a noise below. It was a fox. He had seen the cheese and wanted it for himself. He smiled cleverly at the crow.

"Oh, lovely crow!" he said. "You are such a beautiful bird. I'm sure you sing sweetly too."

The crow was very pleased. She believed the fox. The crow was so keen to show she had a delightful voice that she opened her beak to sing. The piece of cheese fell to the ground. The fox quickly gobbled up the cheese. He looked up at the crow, grinning widely.

"Thank you," he said. "You may have a wonderful voice, but you certainly have no brains!"

- Find all the words that end with **-ed**, **-ful** and **-ly**.
  Write the words you find under the correct headings
  below. Some have already been done for you.

ed	ly	ful
carried	lovely	beautiful

Dear Helper,

Objective: to be able to identify words with particular endings.
Read the story, which is one of Aesop's fables, with your child. Help your child to find all the words ending in -ed, -ly and -ful and underline them in the story. Now ask your child to write the words in the correct columns.

How does it end?

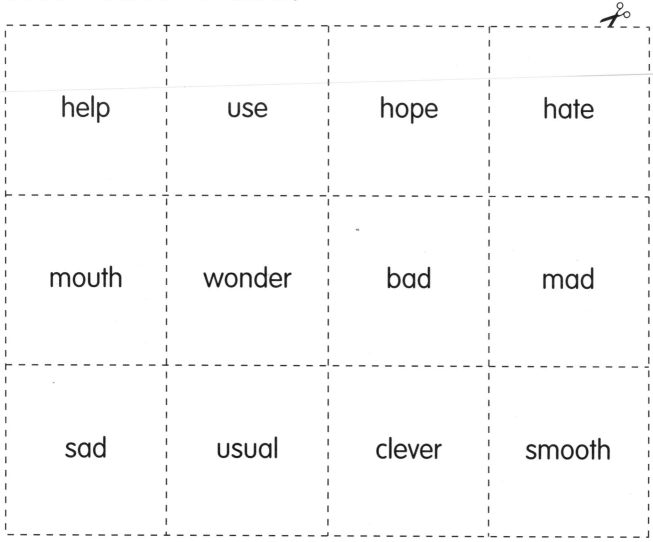

help	use	hope	hate
mouth	wonder	bad	mad
sad	usual	clever	smooth

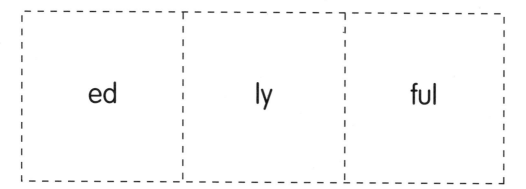

ed	ly	ful

- Read the words above.
- Now cut out the words and the word endings.
- Make new words by choosing an ending that fits.

Dear Helper,

Objective: to add endings to words to make new words.
Help your child to try different word endings with each word root. Talk about the need for the words to make sense: eg 'madful' is not a word, but 'hopeful' is.

What's in a word?

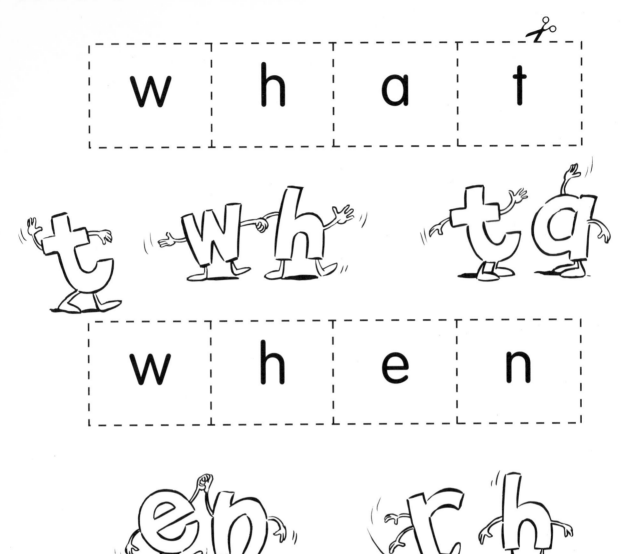

- Read these **wh** question words.
- Can you find any words inside these words? Look carefully and write the words you find.

Dear Helper,

Objective: to be able to spell words beginning with *wh-*.

Help your child to cut out the letters from each word and see if they can find other words, eg 'hat' and 'at' in 'what'. Looking closely at words within words helps children to learn to spell words, especially words that are commonly misspelled, such as these. They can write words they find on a separate sheet of paper.

Words within words

- Look carefully at the words below. Find any words hidden inside them. Try mixing up the letters in each longer word to find other words. Some have been done for you.

- When you have finished finding words, check that you can spell the whole word correctly.

anything _____ any, thing, thin, ant _____

happened _____

giant _____

managed _____

fortune _____

discover _____

frightened _____

careful _____

Dear Helper,

Objective: to learn to spell unfamiliar words.
This activity requires your child to look closely at the letters in each word, which will help them to remember how to spell them. Look first for words without jumbling the letters. If your child finds these quite easily, you can also try using the individual letters in the words to make further words.

PHOTOCOPIABLE

Spelling difficult words

- **Look** at the word carefully, **say** the word aloud, then **cover** the word while you try and **write** the word. Now **check** to see if it is right.

Look, Say, Cover	Write	Check
information		
fiction		
illustration		
diagram		
dictionary		
explanation		
instruction		
caption		
label		
author		

Dear Helper,

Objective: to learn to spell common words.

Help your child to spell these words by looking carefully at the letters in a word, particularly any tricky parts, and then saying the word aloud. They should then fold the paper so that the word is covered. Now encourage them to write the word. Lastly they should check their writing against the printed word.

Where does it belong?

- Look at the list of words below. They need to be put in the correct sections of a catalogue. Write the words in the sections on the grid in alphabetical order.

hairdryers   jewellery   sofas   jigsaw puzzles   school uniforms
shoes   footballs   washing machines   bicycle   umbrellas
pillows   slide   dresses   tables
dolls   cots   gloves   high chairs

Accessories	
Baby equipment	
Children's clothes	
Electrical equipment	
Furniture	
Ladies' fashions	
Sports equipment	
Toys	

Dear Helper,

Objective: to be able to match words to correct alphabetical sections.

Look at the list of words and help your child to match them to the correct section, eg washing machines to electrical equipment. If there is more than one item for a section, help your child to put them into alphabetical order.

The language of books

- Look carefully at the book cover and read the labels.

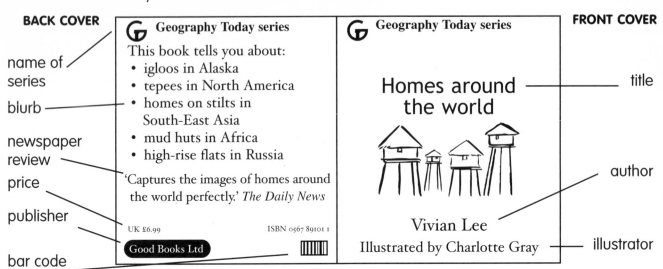

BACK COVER

name of series

blurb

newspaper review

price

publisher

bar code

G Geography Today series

This book tells you about:
- igloos in Alaska
- tepees in North America
- homes on stilts in South-East Asia
- mud huts in Africa
- high-rise flats in Russia

'Captures the images of homes around the world perfectly.' *The Daily News*

UK £6.99   ISBN 0567 89101 1

Good Books Ltd

G Geography Today series

Homes around the world

Vivian Lee

Illustrated by Charlotte Gray

FRONT COVER

title

author

illustrator

- Now write your definition of the words in the grid below.

What do the words mean?	
title	
author	
illustrator	
publisher	
blurb	
bar code	
price	

Dear Helper,

Objective: to be able to define words relating to book covers.

Knowing the meaning of book-related words will help your child to talk about books more easily and to understand the information given on book covers. Look carefully at the picture of the book cover with your child and read the labels. Then help your child write the meanings of the terms in the grid.

It's a match!

excited	expensive	coach
trip	people	water
travel	check	seaside
to feel very interested	cost a lot of money	a bus that takes people on long journeys
a short journey	men, women and children	something you drink that falls from the sky as rain
to go from one place to another	to make sure it is right	a place by the sea

- Read the words and meanings on the cards.
- Now cut the cards out.
- Play a pairs game with your helper, matching the word to its meaning. The winner is the one with the most cards at the end.

Dear Helper,

Objective: to be able to match definitions to words.

Help your child to read all the words and definitions carefully. Cut out the cards and play a pairs game. Turn the cards face down and spread them out. Take turns with your child to turn over two cards at a time. If they match, keep them. The winner is the person with the most pairs at the end.

Write a dictionary page

- Look at the words and meanings below. The words have the wrong meanings. Match each word to its correct meaning and write them in the dictionary page. Make sure they are in alphabetical order. One has been done for you.

- See if you can add some of your own words.

Word	Meaning
excited	a bus that takes people on long journeys
water	a place by the sea
coach	costs a lot of money
check	something you drink that falls from the sky as rain
people	to make sure it is right
expensive	to feel very interested
travel	men, women and children
seaside	a short journey
trip	to go from one place to another

Word	Meaning
check	to make sure it is right

Dear Helper,

Objective: to be able to write a dictionary page of definitions.

Help your child to write the words in alphabetical order and with corresponding definitions using the format above.

Match the meaning

- Look carefully at the lists of words. Draw a line to connect the words that share the same meaning. One has been done for you.

habitat	meat-eating
diet	dead
types	hunted animal
extinct	food
prey	kinds
hibernate	plant-eating
vegetarian	home
carnivorous	sleep through winter

Dear Helper,

Objective: to match words and phrases that express the same or similar meanings.

Help your child to match the words to the correct meanings. You may like to help your child look up some of the unfamiliar words in a dictionary.

PHOTOCOPIABLE

In the past

- Rewrite the sentences in the past tense. The first one has been done for you.

1 Mrs Jones is going to the market.

Mrs Jones went to the market.

2 Edward helps a neighbour.

3 The girl takes a plant to her mother.

4 Jonathan plays dominoes.

5 Salma makes a cake.

6 The dog jumps over the fence.

Dear Helper,

Objective: to be able to write in the past tense.

Help your child to read the sentences and then put them in the past tense (remind your child that this means that the event happened before). If they are having difficulty, suggest they say their new sentences aloud, saying 'Yesterday...' at the beginning of each one.

Name:

Matching past and present

- Look carefully at the verbs (action words). Match up the verbs in the present to those in the past.
  One has been done for you.

Present	**Past**
buy	slept
make	bought
teach	swam
sleep	went
feel	came
swim	taught
grow	felt
bring	dug
go	got
come	made
get	took
see	wanted
run	saw
want	ran
take	brought
dig	grew

Dear Helper,

Objective: to be able to match verbs in the present and past tense.

Read the list of past and present verbs with your child and help them to match the words by drawing lines to the corresponding verbs. If your child is having difficulty, try putting the words into sentences, for example: 'Today I run to school', 'Yesterday I ran to school'.

PHOTOCOPIABLE

Cartoons

- Read the extract and see if you can find names of places and people. We call these proper nouns.
  Underline them all and then write a list in the space below.

A **cartoon** is a picture that is drawn to make people laugh. The word cartoon comes from Italy. There are many different kinds of cartoon.

Walt Disney, who lived in America, made cartoon movies famous. In 1928 he created the most famous cartoon character, Mickey Mouse. Soon after came Donald Duck. Although Disney died in 1966, his movies are still popular with children all over the world, from the United States to China, from Australia to Greenland.

Comic strips are another form of cartoon. They tell a story in a series of pictures. Characters such as Snoopy the dog and Garfield the cat appear in newspapers. Children often read comic books about superheroes such as Superman, Spiderman and Batman. In the United Kingdom, very young children enjoy Rupert the Bear.

Some cartoons make jokes about famous people. Gerald Scarfe is a well-known cartoonist who lives in England. Daumier was the name of a cartoonist who lived in France a long time ago.

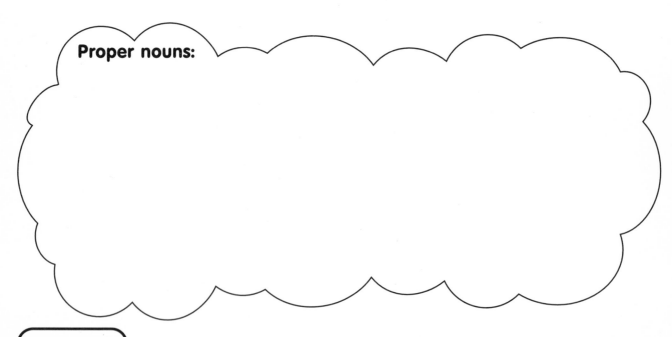

Proper nouns:

Dear Helper,

Objective: to be able to identify proper nouns.

Read the extract with your child and help them to find all the capital letters for names and places. Remind them that a proper noun is the name of a specific person, place or thing and begins with a capital letter. Use their own name as an example.

PHOTOCOPIABLE

The question mark challenge

- Read the conversation between Hannah, who is three years old, and her mother. The computer has taken out all the question marks. Can you put them back? Write above the words.

"What time are Aunty Wendy and Uncle David coming, Mummy"

"About 5 o'clock," said Mum.

"How long is that" asked Hannah.

"About two hours' time," replied Mum, trying to make the bed.

"I might be shy," said Hannah.

"Why" asked Mum. "You remember them, don't you"

Hannah was thoughtful for a moment, before asking another

question. "What colour is their car" said Hannah.

"Blue," said Mum. "Now, stop asking questions."

"Why" said Hannah.

"Because I'm trying to get things done," said Mum.

"Why" said Hannah.

"Oh, stop saying 'Why'," said Mum.

"Why"

"Why are you called Hannah" replied Mum after a while.

"Because I am," said Hannah.

"Why is the world round, then"

"BECAUSE IT IS!" shouted Hannah.

"Now, can we get on" asked Mum.

Dear Helper,

Objective: to be able to punctuate questions correctly.

Read the text with your child, encouraging plenty of expression. You may like to ask your child to read Hannah's part and you read the mother. Now see if you can help your child to put in all the missing question marks.

Talking to the giant

- Read carefully what the giant and Jack are saying.
- Put the missing full stops, question marks and exclamation marks into the speech bubbles.

Dear Helper,

Objective: to be able to use question marks and exclamation marks correctly.

Ask your child to look carefully at the pictures and read the words in the speech bubbles with expression. Talk about the correct punctuation and help them to write it in. You can also help them to write the speech out using speech marks and correct punctuation on the back of the sheet.

Reading detectives

- Look at the list of words. Some of them might be difficult to read and understand.

- Now read the story and look for each word that you read in the list. Read the whole sentence. Can you read and understand the words now?

tortoise	**whole**	**promise**	**squash**	**cheat**
tin-opener	**corned**	**ought**	**plodded**	

There were once three tortoises – a father, a mother and a baby. One fine day they decided to go for a picnic. They chose a place in the woods and they packed tins of salmon, corned beef, sandwiches and orange squash. In about three months they were ready.

They walked and walked and finally, after about a year and a half, they were halfway. They set off again after a rest and, in three years, they reached the picnic place. They unpacked the food. Then Mother Tortoise said, "We've forgotten the tin-opener!"

Mother and Father both said, "You'll have to go back for it, Baby."

"What me? All that way?" said Baby.

"Yes, we'll wait for you."

"Do you promise not to start without me?" asked Baby Tortoise.

"We promise," said Mother and Father Tortoise.

So Baby plodded off through the bushes. Mother and Father got very hungry as they waited and waited, first a whole year, then another and another. They kept on waiting and finally Mother Tortoise said, "It's six years now. Baby Tortoise ought to be back by now."

"Yes, let's just have one sandwich while we are waiting," said Father.

They were just about to pick up the sandwiches when they heard a voice.

"Aha! I knew you'd cheat." And Baby Tortoise popped his head out of a bush. "It's a good thing I didn't start out for that tin-opener," he said.

Dear Helper,

Objective: to be able to read unfamiliar words by using the context.

Look carefully at the words with your child. Then read the story. Discuss why it is funny. Now help your child to scan the story for the words. Help your child to read the whole sentence surrounding the word and discuss how they can work out many unknown words in this way.

It was only yesterday

- Read the story below with your helper and then retell it, keeping it in the past tense.

Emma was feeling much happier today. Yesterday had been a big day for her. For the very first time she had managed to talk in front of the whole class. Emma had not been at the school very long. She had just moved from Scotland and left all her friends behind. Hardest of all was that now she lived with her mum and did not see her dad often, or her grandparents. She particularly missed her grandad. He sometimes seemed the only one who understood how she felt.

Emma had found it very hard to make friends with the children at her new school. They laughed at her funny accent, and at playtimes she usually walked round the playground on her own. She was even shyer in class and hardly ever said anything.

This term all the children had to take turns to bring in a special object to talk about to the class. Emma had made excuses and tried to avoid taking her turn, but finally the time came when Emma's teacher told her it was her turn. Emma had pleaded that she didn't have anything special to show, not like some of the other children. Her teacher said it did not need to be anything amazing, but something special to her. She told Emma about a special necklace that her grandmother had given her. Every time she looked at it, it reminded her of her grandmother. That gave Emma an idea.

The next day Emma came to school clutching a small object wrapped in paper. When the teacher said, "Now, it's Emma's turn," Emma stood up timidly and went to fetch the object from her drawer. Slowly she unwrapped the object and the class gazed in anticipation. As Emma stared at the small object she seemed to gain confidence and began to speak.

"This was my grandad's tobacco tin," she began to explain. She opened the lid and sniffed it and, as she carefully passed it around for the class to smell, she explained how that smell was special to her. Emma described her grandad, how he always had a funny tobacco smell, but how he talked to her and knew just how she felt. She talked about the things they did together, such as helping him at his allotment. Suddenly this shy girl changed to the whole class. Everyone felt as if they knew her grandfather when she had finished, and her teacher just looked in amazement. The class all clapped and for the first time Emma felt she belonged.

At playtime lots of children crowded round her and wanted to talk to her and she began to make friends. That night she wrote a letter to her grandad and told him all about it. He didn't seem so far away now.

Dear Helper,

Objective: to be able to retell a story in the past tense.
This activity will help your child to recall a story and tell it in the past tense. Read the story with them and talk about the main events. Now help them to retell the story, ensuring they keep it in the past tense.

100 LITERACY HOMEWORK ACTIVITIES • YEAR 2 TERM 3

I saw a...

• Read the poem. Each of the lines has got muddled.
Sort them out, then answer the questions.

As in a dream,
I saw a beach that glittered and gleamed,
I saw a ring stuck on a beard,
I saw a pea that looked weird,
I saw a head made of lead,
I saw a pipe spreading butter on bread,
I saw a woman reach up to the sky,
I saw a thread and I wondered why,
I saw all these things.

Where was the pea?

_____

What was the pipe made of?

_____

Who was spreading the butter?

_____

What was reaching up to the sky?

_____

Dear Helper,

Objective: to be able to read with understanding.

The lines in the poem have been muddled – half of each line has moved up to the previous line. Try and help your child to unmuddle it by moving down the second part of the line, eg 'I saw a beach as in a dream, I saw a ring that glittered and gleamed...'. Now help your child to answer the questions.

The school trip

• Read the story and answer the questions.

Alex was excited. Today was the day they were going on the school trip to the seaside. He had been a few times before, but his mum did not have a car, so they had to go on a coach and it was much too expensive to go often. He was soon dressed, had eaten his breakfast and was nagging Mum to take him to school.

"Not yet, Alex. It's not time. Now just make sure you have got everything – packed lunch, drink, spending money and a pair of shorts and hat in case it is hot."

Alex made sure for the hundredth time that it was all there in his bag and, at last, it was time to go. As soon as he got to school, he saw the coach waiting. Some of the others were already waiting in the playground and Mrs Gray, his teacher, was checking she had everything, including the sick bucket!

Finally they were on their way! Alex sat next to Simon, his best friend, and everything was going according to plan. He had no idea how badly it was all going to turn out.

Why was it special for Alex to go to the seaside? _____

Who did Alex live with? _____

What did Alex have to remember to take with him? _____

What was Alex's teacher called? _____

What did Alex's teacher remember to put on the bus? _____

What was Alex's best friend called? _____

Dear Helper,

Objective: to be able to answer questions on a story.
Read the story with your child and then read the questions together. Help your child to write the answers, remembering to write in full sentences.

Name:

The tortoises' picnic

- Read the folk tale below and answer the questions.

There were once three tortoises – a father, a mother and a baby. One fine day they decided to go for a picnic. They chose a place in the woods and they packed tins of salmon, corned beef, sandwiches and orange squash. In about three months they were ready.

They walked and walked and finally, after about a year and a half, they were halfway. They set off again after a rest and, in three years, they reached the picnic place. They unpacked the food. Then Mother Tortoise said, "We've forgotten the tin-opener!"

Mother and Father both said, "You'll have to go back for it, Baby."

"What me? All that way?" said Baby.

"Yes, we'll wait for you."

"Do you promise not to start without me?" asked Baby Tortoise.

"We promise," said Mother and Father Tortoise.

So Baby plodded off through the bushes. Mother and Father got very hungry as they waited and waited, first a whole year, then another and another. They kept on waiting and finally Mother Tortoise said, "It's six years now. Baby Tortoise ought to be back by now."

"Yes, let's just have one sandwich while we are waiting," said Father. They were just about to pick up the sandwiches when they heard a voice.

"Aha! I knew you'd cheat." And Baby Tortoise popped his head out of a bush. "It's a good thing I didn't start out for that tin-opener," he said.

What did the tortoises take on their picnic? _____

Where did they decide to go? _____

Why did it take them so long? _____

What did they forget to take? _____

Where had Baby Tortoise been for six years? _____

Dear Helper,

Objective: to be able to answer questions on a text.

Read the story with your child. Talk about what happened and help them to answer the questions. Some of the answers are not stated directly in the story, so your child will have to think about the questions carefully.

Sack and the Jeanstalk

- Read this funny extract from the story of Sack and the Jeanstalk.
- Underline all the words that are wrong. Then rewrite the correct story of Jack and the Beanstalk next to the pictures.

Once upon a line there was a boy called Jack.
He lived with his mother in a little mouse.
Jack's mother was a poor window.
Now Jack was a very lazy toy.

One day all they had left was the cow.
So Jack took the sow to market to sell her.

On the way he met a man.
"Would you swap your cow for these magic jeans?"
"Oh yes," said Jack.

Dee Reid

_____
_____
_____

_____
_____
_____

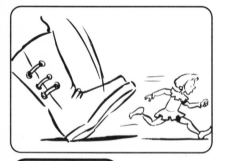

_____
_____
_____

Dear Helper,

Objective: to write sentences to fit a known story.

Read the alternative version of Jack and the Beanstalk and ask your child to underline all the wrong words. Now talk about the well-known, original story and ask your child to look carefully at the pictures depicting the beginning, middle and end of the story. Help them to write sentences to fit each picture.

The school trip – how does it end?

● Read the story with your helper.

Alex was excited. Today was the day they were going on the school trip to the seaside. He had been a few times before, but his mum did not have a car, so they had to go on a coach and it was much too expensive to go often. He was soon dressed, had eaten his breakfast and was nagging Mum to take him to school.

"Not yet, Alex. It's not time. Now just make sure you have got everything – packed lunch, drink, spending money and a pair of shorts and hat in case it is hot."

Alex made sure for the hundredth time that it was all there in his bag and, at last, it was time to go. As soon as he got to school, he saw the coach waiting. Some of the others were already waiting in the playground and Mrs Gray, his teacher, was checking she had everything, including the sick bucket!

Finally they were on their way! Alex sat next to Simon, his best friend, and everything was going according to plan. He had no idea how badly it was all going to turn out.

● Now write what happens next. You can use the back of this sheet. Think about what could have gone wrong and why.

Dear Helper,

Objective: to be able to write an ending to a story.
Talk with your child about a possible ending and encourage them to use their imagination. Did Alex get lost? Did someone get hurt? How did Alex feel and what did he do?

Alliterative sentences

- Look at the pictures of characters and read the list of names, adjectives and verbs.

- Write a silly sentence about each character with lots of words that have the same sound at the beginning. One has been done for you.

Characters	Adjectives	Verbs
Belinda the baby	beautiful	bawls
Winnie the witch	wicked	watches
Bill the burglar	beastly	bumps
Pete the pirate	perfect	paints
Fiona the fairy	funny	fusses
Tilly the teacher	tidy	taps

1 Belinda the beautiful baby bawls behind the building.

2 _____

3 _____

4 _____

5 _____

6 _____

Dear Helper,

Objective: to be able to play with sounds in words to make particular effects.

Look carefully at the pictures of the characters and then read the list of names, adjectives and verbs. Now help your child to put these together into sentences. It does not matter if they do not make sense. That makes them more fun!

Fact or fiction?

Tigers	**The Tiger's Party**
Tigers stalk their prey through thick undergrowth. They sometimes pull their dead prey near to water, because they need to drink plenty during meals. They are unlike most cats because they do not mind water. They eat about 18 kilograms of meat a day.	All the tigers were getting excited, for today was going to be a special day. They were having a party. They were going to eat meat in paper cases, meat on sticks, meat in pastry cases and, best of all, deep-fried meat sticks with tomato ketchup! There would be lots of ice-cold water to drink, too.
Dinosaur Games	**Maiasaurs**
Derek the dangerous dinosaur was on the prowl for something to eat. He poked his long neck around the tree and whooped in delight. Lovely green leaves! But just as he was about to pull some out of the tree, he heard a noise. "Oy, get off! They're mine," said a little voice. To Derek's amazement, a tiny mouse was scampering up the tree. How he ended up playing games with a mouse, he didn't know, but it certainly was fun.	Maiasaurs were middle-sized dinosaurs. They lived in huge herds and were hunted by other dinosaurs. They ate a lot of leaves and plants and kept moving around to find food. Each mother laid about 24 eggs in her nest. A baby maiasaur weighed 1 kilogram when it was born and was about 35 centimetres long. When they were fully grown, maiasaurs were up to 9 metres long and weighed the same as four crocodiles.

- Read the extracts from fiction (story books) and non-fiction (books that tell you facts).

- Cut them out and stick them onto a separate piece of paper in two columns, one for fiction and another for non-fiction.

Dear Helper,

Objective: to be able to distinguish fact from fiction.

Read the above extracts with your child. Talk about whether each one is fiction and tells a story, or gives facts and is non-fiction. Ask your child to cut them into separate sections and then stick them onto a separate piece of paper, with fiction on one side and non-fiction on the other. Help them to write a heading for each column.

Five Ws: who, where, when, what, why?

- Play 'Consequences' with your helper (and other members of your family if you can). Here's how:

1 Each player writes a series of **who**, **where**, **when**, **what**, **why** questions on a piece of paper, similar to those below.

2 Each player then passes their paper to the player next to them.

3 That person writes an answer to the first question and folds the paper to cover the answer.

4 They then pass the paper to another player, who does the same with the next question.

5 Continue to pass the papers until all the questions have been answered.

6 When you have finished, read out the whole thing. You may get some very strange (and funny) stories!

WHO?   Who is the first character? (for example a girl's name)
              Who is the second character? (for example a boy's name)

WHERE?   Where did they meet?

WHEN?   When did they meet

WHAT?   What happened when they met? What did they say to each other?

WHY?   Why did they like or not like each other?

Who is the first character?
    The Queen
Who is the second character?
    Timmy
Where did they meet?
    At the circus
When did they meet?
    In 2020
What happened when they met?
    It rained
Why did they like each other?
    Because they both had freckles

Dear Helper,

Objective: to be able to write suitable questions.

Help your child to write questions similar to those above, and have fun writing silly answers!

Find the telephone number

- Look in a telephone directory at home, and see if you can find telephone numbers for people with these names.

Name	Telephone number
Williams, J	
Davies, M	
Smith, J	
Jones, S	
Andrews, R	
Gardner, N	
Baker, F	
Reed, J	
Arnold, T	
Barrett, P	
Knight, M	
Mathew, R	
Patel, M	
Evans, R	
Clark, L	
Fletcher, J	
Hall, M	
Powell, P	
Thompson, M	
Taylor, N	

Dear Helper,

Objective: to be able to locate information in an index.

A telephone directory is a type of alphabetical index. Help your child to practise alphabetical order skills and scanning for specific information by looking up these names in a telephone directory. They need to write the corresponding telephone number in the right-hand column. Don't worry if your directory doesn't have answers for all of these.

Name:

Find out where

- Answer the questions by looking carefully in the index below. Remember to use alphabetical order to find the word you are looking for.

All About Pets

Index

B	budgerigars	9, 10
C	cats	15, 16
D	dogs	21, 22
F	fish	19, 20
G	gerbils	3, 4
	guinea pigs	2, 3
H	hamsters	1, 2
M	mice	4, 5
P	parrots	17, 18
S	snakes	23, 24

1 Which pages will you look at to find out about goldfish? _____

2 Which pages will tell you about a more dangerous pet? _____

3 Which pages will I look at if I would like a bird as a pet? _____

4 Which pages will tell me about pets that live in water? _____

5 Which pages will tell me about pets that have bright-coloured feathers? _____

Dear Helper,

Objective: to be able to find information from an index.

Help your child to read the question carefully, and remind them to scan their eyes down the index to find the appropriate information.

Make an index

- An index is in alphabetical order with page numbers next to different items. Look carefully at the list of toys below, put them into alphabetical order and write them with the page numbers, which are in brackets, in the grid.

trains (2)
paper aeroplanes (6)
model kits (12)
computer games (9, 10, 11)
dolls (4, 5)
outdoor toys (28, 29, 30)

Lego (7, 8)
jigsaws (15)
board games (16, 17)
cards (18)
action man figures (3)
baby toys (31, 32)

dressing-up clothes (20, 21)
costumes (19)
cars (22, 23)
books (24, 25, 26)
sand toys (27)

Toy	Page numbers

- You have now made your own index for a book on toys! Check that it is in alphabetical order.

Dear Helper,

Objective: to be able to make a short index in alphabetical order.

Help your child to sort the names of the toys into alphabetical order and to write them in the grid, putting the page numbers in the right-hand column.

PHOTOCOPIABLE

Name:

Cover story

- Look at these book covers. Then complete the grid below.

This book tells you about:	
• weather around the world • blizzards • hurricanes • tornadoes	**Weather** Ivor Storm Illustrated by S K Y Blue

This book tells you about:	
• 2-D shapes • 3-D shapes • making shapes • shape patterns	**Shapes** R U Square Illustrated by P E N Tagon

This book tells you about:	
• fashion through the ages • fabrics • designing clothes • making clothes	**Clothes** C L Rail Illustrated by T Shirt

This book tells you about:	
• ants • beetles • bees • buterflies • life cycles	**Insects** A N Ant Illustrated by Tony Beetle

Name of book	Information contained
Clothes	
	number of body parts antennae feeding habits
Weather	
	cylinders, triangles making a pyramid repeating patterns

Dear Helper,

Objective: to be able to find information from book covers.

Look carefully at the book covers above and ask your child to read about what each book contains. Help your child to fill in the grid and encourage them to add extra ideas, based on the back cover information, when they are writing in the second column.

Noting the facts

- Read the extract below about dinosaurs called maiasaurs.
- Fill in the grid to make some notes about the key facts.

Maiasaurs

Maiasaurs were medium-sized dinosaurs that lived about 75 million years ago. Fossils have been found in the state of Montana in the United States of America. The fossils and other remains have told scientists a lot about maiasaurs. They lived in huge herds and were hunted by other dinosaurs, such as the tyrannosaurs. Maiasaurs ate a lot of leaves and plants and kept moving around to find food. Each mother laid about 24 eggs in her nest. A baby maiasaur weighed 1 kilogram when it was born and was about 35 centimetres long. When they were fully grown, they were up to 9 metres long and weighed approximately 2 tonnes, the same as four crocodiles.

Facts about Maiasaurs	
Size when fully grown	
Weight when fully grown	
What they ate	
How the young were born	
What size they were when they were born	
Which country fossils have been found in	

Dear Helper,

Objective: to be able to make notes from a non-fiction text.

Help your child to read the extract all the way through first. Then support them in scanning the text carefully to find the particular information to put into the boxes.

PHOTOCOPIABLE

Name _____

Year 2 Homework Diary

Name of activity	Date sent home	Child's comments		Teacher's comments
		Did you like this? Draw a face. 🙂 a lot 🙂 a little 🙁 not much	**How much did you learn?** Draw a face. 🙂 a lot 🙂 a little 🙁 not much	